The many GĪTĀS in ŚRĪMAD BHĀGAVATAM

Dr. V. GOURI SURESH

The many GĪTĀS in ŚRĪMAD BHĀGAVATAM

Dr. V. GOURI SURESH

Indus Source Books

Indian Spirit, Universal Wisdom

Indus Source Books
PO Box 6194
Malabar Hill PO
Mumbai 400 006
INDIA
Email: info@indussource.com
www.indussource.com

THE MANY GĪTĀS IN ŚRĪMAD BHĀGAVATAM

ISBN: 978-93-85509-64-3

First published by Indus Source Books in 2021

Cover painting: G.S. Praveena Manoj

Cover design: Sanskruti Graphics, Byculla; 9819840840

Printed at Shefali Arts, Bandra, Mumbai 400050

CONTENTS

PREFACE

The human mind is always restless. It is the seat of thoughts, which comes and goes one after the other in never ending succession. When one's mind is thus restless, one can never concentrate on anything. If one can keep his mind calm, one can contemplate on God without distraction. The best method to do this is practising devotion to the Supreme Being. When one has controlled his mind, he is not affected by the words or actions of anyone. There is nothing that such a man cannot achieve. He is not scared of anything – not even death. He knows that just like dreams appear to be real when one is asleep, the whole world seems to be real as long as one is ignorant. When he gains true knowledge, he realises that the whole world is actually virtual. Nothing else exists except the Supreme Being. Everything else has been formed from Him and will dissolve into Him. This fundamental truth is emphasised over and over again throughout Śrīmad Bhāgavatam or the Bhāgavat Purāna.

There are many Gītās in Bhāgavat Purāna. The first one is Kapilagīta, which occurs in the third canto. Here, we see Sage Kapila, an incarnation of Lord Viṣṇu, advising his mother on the importance of developing Vairāgya or dispassion in life. Rudragīta, seen towards the end of the fourth canto, comprises the advice given by Rudra to ten brother princes on worshipping

Lord Mahāviṣnu. Next is the Yamagīta of the seventh canto. Here, Yama, the God of Death, is seen explaining the meaninglessness of grieving over death, as death is unavoidable, and anyone who is born has to die.

The next seven Gītās, namely Veṇugīta, Gopikāgīta, Yugalagīta, Virahagīta, Bhrāmaragīta, Śrutigīta, and Mahiṣigīta are seen in the tenth canto. The first five of these are sung by Gopikās, devotees of the highest order of Lord Kṛṣṇa. They are in fact jīvātmās, who are always in search of the Paramātma. They experience limitless joy when they succeed in their search. In fact, this merger is the ultimate aim of every human being. Śrutigīta comprises the answers given by Sage Śuka to specific questions put by King Parīkṣit. This Gīta, based purely on knowledge contained in the Vedās, is also part of the tenth canto. Mahiṣigīta is sung by the queens of Kṛṣṇa, illustrating their fondness to him.

In addition to these, the eleventh canto of Śrīmad Bhāgavatam has many Gītās. The latter part of this canto is in the form of a detailed question-answer session, which is the famous Uddhavagīta. The one who put the questions was Uddhava, one of the greatest devotees of Lord Kṛṣna. The one who answered the questions was Kṛṣna himself. In conclusion, Lord Kṛṣna advised Uddhava to shun the thoughts of 'I' and 'mine', and see the whole world as the seat of God. He told Uddhava that by practising this 'adhyātma yoga', he could become one with the Supreme Being.

Within the Uddhavagīta, there are three separate sets of verses, relating a story each, used by Lord Kṛṣna to explain his point. These are the Haṁsagīta, Bhikṣugīta and Ailagīta.

Reading, understanding and contemplating on the ideas and ideals contained in these Gītās will provide everlasting happiness to mankind. I consider myself truly fortunate and blessed by the Almighty as I am about to begin this work with humility and devotion. In this humble work, though the concerned Sanskrit verses are not given in original, meanings of all of them are given briefly, along with the respective reference numbers; these obviously remain the same in compilations and interpretations by all authors.

For the verse numbers quoted in this book, I have referred to Śrīmad Bhāgavatam by Sahitya Kesari Late Sri. Pundit P. Gopalan Nair (Volumes 1 to 8) published in 2009 as Third Edition by Guruvayur Devaswam, Kerala, India. For concerned stories given as introduction to the chapters, I have taken short excerpts from my own book *Stories from Bhaagavatham* published by Bharatiya Vidya Bhavan in 2004. For the hidden meanings of the verses of Gopikāgīta, reference has been made to *Saṁpūrṇa Bhāgavata Rahasyam* by Swāmi Jñāñānanda Saraswati, published by Anandakuteeram, Kanyakumari, in 1992.

I hereby seek the forgiveness of all my learned readers for any error that might have crept into this work inadvertently. If they find this book helpful in guiding them at all times, and also in enhancing their spirituality, leading to everlasting bliss and peace, I shall consider myself blessed indeed.

Salutations to Lord Śrī Kṛṣna, the Master of the Universe!

Om Namo Nārāyaṇāya!

Om Namo Bhagavate Vāsudevāya!

NOTE FOR PRONUNCIATION

As is well known, it is difficult to correctly pronounce proper nouns and other words in Sanskrit when they are written in the English language. To overcome this difficulty, all such words are transliterated in the present work, using international dia-critical marks. This code is given below for the readers to refer to, as and when needed.

STANDARD INTERNATIONAL TRANSLITERATION CODE

(Used to transliterate Sanskrit words in the text)

अ	आ	इ	ई	उ	ऊ
a	ā	i	ī	u	ū
ए	ऐ	ओ	औ	अं	अः
e	ai	o	au	ṁ	ḥ
क	ख	ग	घ	ङ	
ka	kha	ga	gha	ṅa	

च	छ	ज	झ	ञ	
ca	cha	ja	jha	ña	
ट	ठ	ड	ढ	ण	
ṭa	ṭha	ḍa	ḍha	ṇa	
त	थ	द	ध	न	
ta	tha	da	dha	na	
प	फ	ब	भ	म	
pa	pha	ba	bha	ma	
य	र	ल	व	श	ष
ya	ra	la	va	śa	ṣa
स	ह	क्ष	त्र	ज्ञ	
sa	ha	kṣa	tra	jña	

INTRODUCTION

Vedās are the most ancient scriptures in the world. They are four in number, namely Ṛgveda, Sāmaveda, Yajurveda and Atharvaveda. In the Hindu epic Mahābhārata, the composition of Vedas is credited to Brahma, the Creator. Vyāsa, son of Sage Parāśara and Satyavati, observed that the knowledge contained in the Vedās was too profound for people to understand. To solve this problem, he explained the Vedās for the benefit of the common man. As a result of this mammoth task, he got the name Vedavyāsa.

Later, different sages in different places and at different times summarised the Vedās into what are known as Upaniṣads. There are twenty-one Upaniṣads based on Ṛgveda, one hundred and nine Upaniṣads on Yajurveda, one thousand on Sāmaveda and fifty on Atharvaveda. Thus the total number of Upaniṣads is one thousand one hundred and eighty. Of these, one hundred and eight are well known, while ten are very popular.

Sage Vedavyāsa, knowing that the verses contained in the Upaniṣads would also be difficult to grasp, explained the meanings of the Vedās and Upaniṣads in the form of interesting stories. These are the Purānās. There are eighteen Purānās, of which Śrīmad Bhāgavatam is the most celebrated, and also the last to be composed. According to Sage Vedavyāsa, Lord Viṣnu himself had explained Bhāgavatam to Lord Brahma, who then narrated it to Sage Nārada. The Sage had later passed it on to him.

Just as predicted by Sage Nārada, Vedavyāsa got everlasting peace of mind after composing the Bhāgavat Purāna. This was but natural, for the real essence of this Purāna is pure, undiluted bhakti. Each canto, each chapter, each verse is immersed in bhakti. The knowledge of all the Vedās is contained in the Bhāgavatam. Reading or even merely listening to this great Purāna, or even narrating it to others, will remove all ignorance from one's mind and will inspire one to lead a virtuous life, dedicating each thought, word and deed to the Lord Supreme.

There are eighteen thousand verses in the Bhāgavatam, organised in twelve cantos. Of these, the tenth canto is the longest; it is here that the life of Lord Kṛṣna is dealt with in detail. In the eleventh canto, the Uddhava Gīta can be seen, which is the advice given by Lord Kṛṣna to his devotee Uddhava, as well as the swargārohan (ascending to heaven) of the Lord, which took place thereafter. Uddhavagīta is very long, spread over more than half of the eleventh canto, and comprising one thousand forty two verses. It starts towards the end of Chapter 6 and extends up to the end of Chapter 29. It includes three separate Gītās within it. Of these, Hamsagīta comprises nineteen verses; Bhikṣhugīta comprises sixteen verses and Ailagīta eighteen. The twelfth canto includes a few stories and the conclusion of the great Purāna.

All the other Gītās in Bhāgavatam are seen in the earlier cantos. The first Gīta appears in the third canto, known as the Kapilagīta. It is very long, and includes 348 verses, spread over eight chapters. Next is the Rudragīta, a collection of thirty eight verses, appearing in the fourth canto. Yamagīta is seen in the seventh canto, covering twenty one ślokās.

The next seven occur in the tenth canto – these are the Veṇugīta of thirteen verses, Gopikāgīta comprising nineteen verses, Yugalagīta of twenty four verses, Virahagīta including thirteen verses, Bhrāmaragīta of ten verses, Śrutigīta of twenty eight, and Mahiṣigīta of ten.

All the Gītās incorporated in Śrīmad Bhāgavatam are greatly beneficial in cleansing the human mind. Furthermore, final liberation from the mortal world is the theme of the eleventh canto. In short, understanding these Gītās and contemplating on them will result in enlightenment and ultimate redemption.

At this juncture, when I am about to start explaining the Gītās in the revered Bhāgavat Purāna based on my limited knowledge, I offer my humble salutations to the Supreme Being for helping me to complete this work successfully.

CHAPTER 1

KAPILAGĪTA

Kardama Prajāpati, one of the sons of Lord Brahma, was a very pious person. He spent his days in austerities and meditation, but his father, the creator, had asked him to marry and lead a householder's life. Kardama was hence in a dilemma. He prayed to Lord Viṣnu and beseeched the Lord to show him a way out.

Nārāyana told him: "Marry Devahūti, Manu's daughter. Both of you can then lead a life of penance. Later, I myself shall be born to you."

Hearing this, Kardama was elated.

One day, Manu went to Lord Brahma and told him how difficult it was to find a match for his daughter Devahūti. Brahma advised him to arrange her marriage with his son, Kardama.

Manu knew that Kardama was a spiritually inclined person, and did not believe in pomp and show. So he took just his wife and daughter to his would be son-in-law's hermitage. Kardama received them appropriately. Manu requested him to marry Devahūti.

Kardama replied: "You know that I would like to lead the life of an ascetic. I am marrying only because my father wishes it. I shall do one thing – I shall marry your daughter, but after we get a son, I will leave her and go back to my penance. If you agree to this condition, I shall do as you say."

Manu and his queen did not know what to say, but the princess agreed to the condition. Thus, the marriage was solemnized in the hermitage of the groom in the dense forest. What a strange marriage!

The beautiful princess now started leading the life of an ascetic herself. She treated Kardama as her preceptor. For twelve years they lived in this way. Then, Kardama blessed her, and for a few years, they lived happily as householders. The first nine children born to them were daughters. The tenth child was a son, and he later became famous as Sage Kapila or Kapila Vāsudeva.

At the birth of Kapila, Devās showered celestial flowers on the earth, Gndharvās played musical instruments and Apsarās danced in the sky. The Creator, along with many Ṛṣis, came down to Kardama's hermitage at the bank of River Saraswati. Brahma congratulated Kardama and told him to get his beautiful and pious daughters married to suitable Ṛṣis who had accompanied him. The Creator congratulated Devahūti also at the birth of her son who, he said, was Mahāviṣṇu incarnated on Earth to teach people Sāṁkhya Śāstra. From him, Devahūti would also learn the same, and ignorance removed, would be a liberated soul.

Saying so, Brahma went back to his abode Satyaloka, along with Nārada, Sanalkumāra and some other Maharṣis. Nine Maharṣis remained in Kardama's Āśram. Soon, they married the nine daughters of Kardama, and took them happily to their respective Āśramās.

After his daughters and sons-in-laws left his Āśram, Kardama approached his son, thanked him profusely for being born to him, congratulated him for planning to popularize Sāṁkhya-Śāstra on Earth and expressed his desire to retire to forest for penance. Taking Kapila's blessings, Kardama gave up his family life and went away for penance.

Devahūti had only her son with her in the hermitage now. Five years passed by. One day, she asked the Lord, "All through my life, I pleased my Indriyās in the hope of getting happiness and satisfaction. However, I did not get any joy or peace of mind. On the contrary, my sorrows have only increased. How can I get permanent peace of mind?"

Lord Kapila Vāsudeva replied, "Mother, try to think of God at all times. If you love God more than anyone and anything else, your mind will get detached from all materialistic things. This is the only way to be eternally blissful."

Thereafter, he explained to his mother the importance of dispassion (vairāgya) in great detail. This part of the Bhāgavat Purāna is famous as Kapilopadeśa (advice given by Kapila). It is also referred to as Kapilagīta. It is very long, extending over nine chapters, from Chapters 25 to 33. The third canto ends with Chapter 33.

The third and fourth cantos of the Bhāgavat Purāna are presented in the form of a dialogue between Sage Maitreya and Vidura. The former was the speaker and the latter, the listener. The entire story of Kardama and Kapila are detailed in the third canto, which ends with the Kapilagīta. Some verses are seen as recited by Sage Maitreya while some depict Devahūti asking questions of her son, Sage Kapila. Others are verses recited by the son in answer to his mother's questions. As Kapila's discourse is very elaborate, covering a vast range of topics, only selected ślokās are being included in this work.

The fifth verse and a few following that, of the twenty fifth chapter of the third canto, set the stage for Kapilopadeśa.

3.25.5: Sage Maitreya said to Vidura, "After Kardama went away to the forest for penance, Bhagwān Kapila remained with his mother to clear her spiritual doubts, which would benefit her immensely.

3.25.6: 'Devahūti remembered the words of Brahma the Creator, and addressed her eminent son, taken birth to illustrate to humanity the right philosophical principles.

3.25.7: "Devahūti said, 'Hé omnipresent Prabho! Let me tell you why I am grieved. I am entwined in this illusory world, because despite my best attempts, I am not able to shrug off my desires and am a slave to my sense organs.

3.25.8: 'I am engulfed in the darkness of this ocean of ignorance; by your blessing, I have now come in contact with you. I have been born many times, but it is only now, after so many births, that I shall be able to see the light of knowledge.

3.25.9: 'You are God Himself who is the cause of this universe; you have taken birth in this world to remove the ignorance of the worldly human beings and infuse the light of knowledge in them.

3.25.10: 'Hé Bhagvān! I am being misguided by the ego in me, which makes me believe that I am my body and that my relations are mine. You are the only one fit to free me from this misunderstanding.

3.25.11: 'My salutations to you, who are the best person that can cut off the roots of the tree that is the world, and lead me to salvation. I am eager to know the truth behind Prakṛti and Puruṣa; I take refuge in you, you who know best what righteousness is and how one can be righteous at all times."

In the next śloka, Maitreya describes the reaction of Sage Kapila to his mother's words.

3.25.12: Maitreya said, "Bhagvān Kapila was happy that his mother asked him such a question, because the answer to this question would be useful to all those who are suffering in various ways and wish to know the path to salvation. In his mind, he congratulated his mother and began his discourse with a smile on his face.

3.25.13: "The Lord said, 'I believe that yoga is the path to salvation, for with the help of yoga, those who want to escape materialism can realize the true nature of the Ātma. It is through knowing the truth about the Ātma that one can overcome the recurrence of sorrows and joys resulting from the materialistic world, escape the cycle of birth and death, and attain Mokṣa.

3.25.14: 'I had once told some Ṛṣis in detail how to practice the eight fold yoga, which is capable of giving one ultimate salvation. I shall now explain the same yoga to you.

3.25.15: 'Mind is the cause of both bondage and salvation. If the mind is attached to senses and desires, bondage will result. However, if it is engaged in thoughts of God, salvation will be the outcome.

3.25.16: 'When the mind is free of negative emotions like lust, greed etc. which arise out of a sense of 'I' and 'mine', joys and sorrows feel the same.

3.25.17: 'If this is the case, then the jīvātma sees the Paramātma which is not connected to anything or anyone, which is different from nature, which cannot be split and is forever self-luminescent.

3.25.18: 'If the mind is wise, detached from the world, and devoted to God, the jīvātma sees the Paramātma which is not indulged in any karma and is indifferent to nature.

3.25.19: 'For yogis, there is no better path to realize the Supreme Being than pure devotion, which unites them with the Lord.

3.25.20: 'The wise know that attachment binds the mind more strongly to desires. This tendency is enhanced by company with bad people; so the wise keep the company of good people and travel along the path to salvation.

3.25.21: 'Those who possess the virtues of patience and magnanimity, who are friends to all, and have no enemies, who are above lust, anger etc., have good habits, and are therefore at peace at all times, are holy people.

3.25.22: 'Those who are strongly devoted to me, without their minds engaged with others, those who give up their karmas and also their near and dear to attain me, are holy people.

3.25.23: 'No type of sorrow affects those who listen to or tell others sacred stories about me, and those whose minds are fixed in me.

3.25.24: 'Hé good natured one! These people, who have given up affection to everyone else except me, are divine. They know the evil consequences of bad company and have succeeded in shunning such company; therefore, you can very well be associated with them.

3.25.25: 'Listening to their discourses on my stories and adventures will be nectar to your ears and will bring happiness to your mind. Association with such holy people will increase love and devotion and affirm faith in the path to salvation.

3.25.26: 'One who contemplates on my deeds will become true devotees and will shun sensual pleasures. Such a person will enthusiastically follow yoga and try to control his mind.

3.25.27: 'Shunning all materialistic desires, he will attain true knowledge. Due to the ensuing devotion to me, he will actualize the Paramātma while still existing as a jīvātma."

In 3.25.28 and 29, Devahūti asks Sage Kapila which form of devotion is the noblest and by doing what she can easily experience the bliss in reaching the state of mokṣa, what the form of the yoga described by him is, and what the subdivisions of this yoga are. In 11.25.30, she requests her son Kapila to make her understand the sāmkhya yoga. She says she is not intelligent enough to grasp its intricacies easily.

In 3.25.31, Maitreya tells Vidura that the Lord, because of his love to his mother, described to Devahūti in detail the meaning of pure devotion to God and the principles of Sāṁkhya Yoga which strengthen that devotion.

3.25.32 and 33: The Lord said, "If a person dedicates all his deeds through all sense organs to God at all times, and makes this his habit, he is a pure devotee. Such a person does not long for any pleasure in this or the other world. For cultivating such total devotion, he will have to do his works purely for pleasing God and not for any other result. Just like fire destroys any fuel, the fire of bhakti will consume the ignorance of he whose mind is fixed on God. At this point, he will experience the ultimate bliss, which is the same as nirvāṇa.

3.25.34: 'Some great devotees are happy and contented in serving me and singing my glory. Who does not cherish a state in which he is united with me?

3.25.35: 'Hé Mother! Such good souls see me, ever ready to fulfill their wishes, and converse with me.

3.25.36: 'Even though they do not desire anything else, as their hearts are filled with love for me, when they leave their bodies, they become one with me.

3.25.37: 'On account of their undiluted devotion, their ignorance is completely destroyed and so they do not care for any siddhis. Such souls who reach my world experience total bliss.

3.25.38: 'Those who reach the world of absolute peace do not have to go through the cycle of birth and death any longer. I am their father, mother, friend, teacher, and god. Therefore, the cycle of time does not affect them.

3.25.39 and 40: 'Some devotees do not desire the pleasures available in this world or the other as they see me in everything. I shall help such people tide over the cycle of birth and death.

3.25.41: 'I am the god of gods and nature; so only those who take refuge in me and in none else can be free of fear (of death and birth).

3.25.42: 'It is due to fear in me that the wind blows, the sun spreads heat, Indra causes rain, fire burns, and Yama does his work.

3.25.43: 'Yogis who are enlightened and dispassionate are devoted to me; they surrender unto my feet as they are free from doubts and fear.

3.25.44: 'Being intensely devoted to me, and fixing mind in me is the only way to achieving all the Puruṣārthās.'

Here ends Chapter 25 of canto three based on Bhakti Yoga. The next chapter elaborates the Sāṁkhya Yoga. Bhagwān Kapila continues:

3.26.1: 'I shall now tell you in detail the principles knowing which one can attain mokṣa.

3.26.2: 'I shall explain to you how knowledge leads to realization of the self. Only by realization of self can one overcome ego.

3.26.3: 'This universe exists because of union with Puruṣa, who is above Guṇās, different from Prakṛti, who is without beginning and is self-luminescent.

3.26.4: 'This Puruṣa received Prakṛti, who had come accidentally to Him. She is the essence of all Sātvik Guṇās and is the power of God.

3.26.5: 'Seeing Prakṛti creating subjects similar to each other and different from each other due to differences in their Guṇās, Jīvan (part of Puruṣa, the other part being Īśwara) was attracted to her.

3.26.6: 'It was because of the mistaken notion about self that Jīvan began taking responsibility for all actions of the body. He began to believe that he does the actions and he gets the results of his actions.

3.26.7: 'Therefore, Jīvan gets bound to the world through body, forgetting that he is not the doer, he is just the observer, and he is in fact pure bliss.

3.26.8: 'The enlightened know that it is because of Prakṛti that Jīvan experiences doer-ship and receiver-ship, whereas it is Puruṣa who is the actual doer and receiver of results.'

At this juncture, the mother Devahūti has a doubt and she seeks clarification of the same. She asks her son Kapila:

3.26.9: 'What are the signs of Prakṛti and Puruṣa, who together create this world?'

Lord Kapila answers this question in great detail. This explanation takes up the rest of this chapter as well as some verses of the next. He says:

3.26.10: 'Prakṛti is the amalgamation of all the three Guṇās, namely Sātvik, Rājasik and Tāmasik. It is not controlled by the sense organs, is without creation and dissolution, is shapeless, is the basis of all, and is a combination of the gross and the subtle. (Prakṛti is not Brahmaṁ, for the latter has no Guṇās.)

3.26.11: 'The wise have realized the importance of the collections of five, five, ten and four forming a distinct group of twenty four.

3.26.12: 'The Earth, water, fire (energy), air, and the sky are the five bhūtās (main elements). Smell, taste, form, touch, and sound form the five tanmātrās (stimuli).

3.26.13: 'The indriyās are ten in number. Jnānendriyās (sense organs) are five – namely nose, tongue, eye, skin and ear, while karmendriyās (organs of work) are also five – mouth, hands, legs, reproductive organ, and defaecator organ. Together, they make ten.

3.26.14: 'The inner organs which are subtle are four in number – manas (mind), budhi (intellect), ahaṁkār (ego), and cittaṁ (memory) together make the antaḥkaraṇa (inner cause or internal organ).

3.26.15-16: 'I say that these are the twenty four tatvās (principles) of brahma. Some say that there is a twenty fifth one, which is time. It is because of its ignorance and ego that Jīvan is afraid of time, which ultimately is the cause of death.

3.26.17: 'Hé daughter of Manu! In fact, what causes the inactive Prakṛti to become active is Bhagwān, and that is time.

3.26.18: 'What exists inside beings as Puruṣa and outside as time is Bhagvān Himself.

3.26.19: 'By the union of Puruṣa and Prakṛti, what was created first was the Mahattatva.

3.26.20: 'The non-destructible Mahattatva was the origin of the world. By its own brilliance, it removed the darkness enveloping the world within it, so that the world became visible.

3.26.21: 'Mahattatva was pure, stable, and sātvik. The four subtle inner organs, namely mind, intellect, ego and memory can be said to be formed from Mahattatva.

3.26.22-32: 'Mahattatva was tranquil initially. When it was disturbed, Ahaṁkāra or Ego was formed. This Ego had three forms – Sātvik, Rājasik and Tāmasik. From Sātvik Ahaṁkāra, manas, i.e. mind was formed; from Rājasik Ahaṁkāra, budhi, i.e. intellect and the ten indriyās (five jnānendriyās and five karmendriyās) were formed. From Tāmasik Ahaṁkāra, the five bhūtās and the five tanmātrās were formed.'

From 3.26.33 to 3.26.72, the characters of all the twenty four tatvās are discussed in detail. This elaborate explanation ends with the last verse, i.e. the seventy second verse of this chapter.

In the twenty seventh chapter of the third canto, the Lord continues thus:

3.27.1: 'Reflection of the sun moves according to the movements of the water while the real sun in the sky looks stationary. Similarly, Jīvan is not affected by the Guṇās of nature as it is beyond Guṇās, is not the doer, and has no emotions.

3.27.2: 'Yet when it is entrapped by senses and sense organs, the 'I'-ness comes into play. This ignorance makes the Jīva think that it is the doer of karmās.

3.27.3: 'Because of this pride in the body, the Jīva enters a cycle and is born again and again in low and high forms of life, based on the bad and good deeds done in each life.

3.27.4: 'The world is an illusion; the Jīva experiences the joys and sorrows in each life just like a person believes his dream to be real as long as he is asleep.

3.27.5: 'Therefore it is of utmost importance to control the mind step by step with the help of strong devotion and detachment.

3.27.6-11: 'One should practice yogic methods like yama, niyama etc., be honest, listen to my stories, treat everyone and everything as equal, shed hatred towards anyone or anything, avoid unnecessary arguments with others, perform one's duties sincerely, and be free of greed. By strictly following the path of morality, being content with whatever one has, by practicing moderate eating, by contemplating on the knowledge gained, by living away from materialism, by controlling the mind, by being a well-wisher of all, by being kind and courageous, and by not succumbing to desires, one can understand the working of Prakṛti and Puruṣa, and experience the real self that is different from the mortal body. Knowing that the self shines in the antaḥkaraṇa, and at the same time is omnipresent, one should remain calm.

3.27.12-13: 'Seeing reflection of the sun in water, one can conclude that there is sun in the sky, and can see it also. Similarly, if one tries to analyze the truth, he will know that real knowledge is hidden due to the presence of the body, senses and mind; within this covering is the real self.

3.27.14-16: 'Ātma or the soul is the one who is awake when the bhūtās, the indriyās, subtle parts like the mind, intellect, ego etc. are in the state of deep slumber. At such times, jīvan imagines that the ego is destroyed, though it is still there; only it is not manifested. The wise know this truth; they know that the mortal body is alive because of the presence of the Paramātma in it.'

In the next four verses, Devahūti asks certain questions to her son Bhagvān Kapila.

3.27.17-20: 'Hé Bhagvān, Hé skillful spiritual teacher! Māya never leaves Jīvan completely. Prakṛti and Puruṣa never leave each other too. Karmās of Jīvās are never extinguished, as they go on accumulating over subsequent lives, even if they are also being burnt continuously. In such a situation, how is ultimate salvation possible?'

Bhagvān Kapila utilizes the twenty first to the thirtieth and last verse of this chapter in clearing his mother's doubt.

3.27.21-30: 'Righteous deeds, pure conscience, deep and longstanding devotion unto me, true knowledge, strong dispassion, yoga with penance, and distraction-less introspection will completely burn away in this lifetime itself the ignorance in which humans live day and night. Māya causes the darkness of ignorance in humans, but once light of knowledge shines, it cannot affect them. Bad dreams seen in sleep disturb people. But once they wake up, they are unaffected while recollecting the same dreams. Similarly, Māya does not affect those whose minds are fixed in me. Those who are absorbed in me, and are fully aware of the real aim of life have no doubts. They have conquered their senses, and are disinterested in this or any other world. Such people attain salvation in this life itself. Hé Mother! Due to prolonged yoga, people achieve various siddhis, but if they get distracted by them, they will not be able to attain me. On the other hand, if they proceed further without getting attracted by siddhis, they attain me and become immortal.'

Here ends the twenty seventh chapter. All the forty four ślokās in the next chapter are spoken by Bhagvān Kapila to his mother Devahūti.

3.28.1: 'Hé daughter of a king! I shall now tell you the nature and characteristics of Sabīja Yoga. By practicing this yoga, a pure mind can recognize the path to God realization.

3.28.2-7: 'By serving noble people with whatever is available to one as a result of his own karma, being interested in the path to liberation, eating clean food moderately, living in undisturbed localities, not cheating anyone, owning only whatever is absolutely essential, practicing celibacy, performing meditation and suitable vratās, maintaining cleanliness, learning scriptures, worshipping God, speaking moderately, controlling senses and prāṇa, pondering on God's līlās, conquering mind which keeps wandering along wrong paths, and shunning inertia, one should slowly and steadily unite with the Supreme Being with the help of his untiring effort.

3.28.8: 'One should select a clean place and spread his sitting mat there. Thereafter, he can sit straight in a comfortable āsana (posture) like the swastika āsana.

3.28.9: 'After that, by practicing prānāyāma through Pūrakam, Kumbhakam, and Recakam, either in this order or in the reverse order, whichever is comfortable, one should purify the path along which the prāṇa travels. This stabilizes the mind.

3.28.10: 'The mind of one who has controlled his breath through this type of prānāyāma is soon freed of rājasik defects like ego, just like fire with the help of air purifies metals like gold.

3.28.11: 'One should burn away diseases by prānāyāma, attraction to sensory objects through pratyāhāra, sins by dhāranās, along with qualities which are obstacles in the path to devotion and worship of God by dhyāna.

3.28.12: 'When the practitioner's mind thus becomes pure by yoga, looking at the tip of his nose, he should meditate on Bhagvān.'

Details of the specific terms are given in the Annexure.

In the next six ślokās, the form of Bhagvān which can be meditated upon is described.

3.28.13-18: 'Face beautiful like an open lotus blossom, eyes slightly reddish like the central part of a red lotus flower, complexion that of a blue lotus, four arms holding conch, discus, mace, and lotus, the head wearing a magnificent crown, the hip adorned by a silk dhoti golden yellow in color similar to the pollen inside a lotus bloom, the chest showing a scar named Śrīvalsam, the neck adorned with a glittering gem called Kaustubham, wearing a long floral garland attracting intoxicated beetles buzzing sweetly, wrists and upper arms with shining bangles, waist adorned by a circlet of gold and gems, lotus-like feet worshipped by the entire mankind – the entire body ever young and enticing, the beautiful form, peaceful and appealing to the eyes and minds of devotees, facial expression showing haste in blessing devotees, famous for the ability to remove the defects in the created world, magnanimous in preserving intact the fame of the noble and pious, sitting in the lotus that is the heart of each devotee. This divine form should be meditated upon without the mind getting distracted. Constant practice of this activity will result in the practitioner achieving the highest degree of concentration power of the mind.

3.28.19: 'Meditate without expecting any reward on this form in any posture – standing, walking, sitting, lying down, doing any charming Līla etc.

3.28.20: 'Once the practitioner is able to concentrate on the entire form successfully without distraction, he should focus on any one part of this form at a time, and then continue with the other parts one after the other without getting distracted.

The next thirteen Ślokās deal with the order in which the various parts of the body should be meditated upon.

3.28.21: 'Firstly, meditate upon Bhagvān's feet with glowing nails, and soles with specific marks of thunderbolt, elephant hook, flag and lotus flower, on them. The light originating from his moon-like toe nails is capable of eliminating the darkness of ignorance from anyone's heart.

3.28.22: 'Meditate on the feet for long, the feet from which the holy Ganga originated initially and later fell on Lord Śiva's head, making him happy.

3.28.23: 'Moving upwards, deliberate on the knees of the Lord which are placed by the lotus eyed Goddess Lakṣmi on her thighs, and which are being caressed by her who is worshipped by Devās.

3.28.24: 'Be conscious of the powerful and blue complexioned thighs of Bhagvān sitting on His vehicle Garuda, and His posterior around which the golden yellow silk fixed in position by a glittering waist band flows till His ankles.

3.28.25: 'Further, fix in mind the Lord's cave-like navel, the cave that contains all the worlds and from which originated the lotus flower, with the Creator sitting on it; and then move upwards to concentrate on His two nipples which shine like two emerald gems and look dark in color due to the pearl necklaces positioned near them.

3.28.26: 'Then meditate on the Lord's chest, where Bhagvati Lakṣmi the goddess of prosperity resides, and His neck which enhances the brilliance of the gem Kaustubham, which is worshipped by devotees all over the world.

3.28.27: 'Next, deliberate on the arms of the Lord, wearing sparkling arm bands, whose luster has been amplified due to contact with the Mandara Mountain during churning of the milky ocean, His discus with intense brilliance, the Sudarśana Cakra which saves people from all danger, and the conch which glows like a divine swan on His lotus-like hand.

3.28.28: 'After that, ponder on Kaumodaki, the mace dear to the Lord that has annihilated many enemies in battle, and His floral garland surrounded by sweetly buzzing bumblebees.

3.28.29: 'Then concentrate intensely on the lotus like face of Bhagvān, who incarnated on Earth to bless His devotees, the face with flawless cheeks reflecting the glitter of His ear ornaments and majestic nose; the face which gives ultimate bliss to devotees.

3.28.30: 'Mediate with full concentration on the Lord's radiant face, with lustrous curls of hair around, with eyes shaped like lotus petals, and with glittering eyebrows.

3.28.31: 'Deliberate on the Lord's smiling eyes that reflect His magnanimity, His readiness to remove the deepest sorrows of devotees with His kind blessings, and His loving glance.

3.28.32: 'Further, reflect profoundly on the smile of Śrī Hari that is enough to dry up the ocean of tears shed by the anguished, which can fulfill any wish of devotees. Ponder on the Lord's beautifully arched eyebrows that can, with a slight movement, defeat the intentions of Manmatha, the God of Love, to swerve even sages from penance.

3.28.33: 'With intense love and devotion, meditate deeply on the smile of Bhagvān Viṣṇu emanating from His lustrous lips, and the two rows of small, shapely and shining teeth; do not think of anything else.

3.28.34: 'In this way, when the heart melts due to intense love of Śrī Hari and ego vanishes due to supreme devotion, the mind is immersed in tears of joy and becomes one with Him.

3.28.35: 'When the mind thus dissolves effortlessly in God, then the Jīvan gets detached wholly from desires and realizes the one and only Ātma.

3.28.36: 'Such realization helps the Jīvan to know the meaninglessness of joy and grief. The fact is that the doer was never he; it was the ego that made him think so.

3.28.37: 'For such a person, this is his last birth. He is not aware of his body. Therefore, he does not experience happiness or sorrow. He will never be born again or die in consequence.

3.28.38: 'Just like one who has woken up from sleep will not think that his dream was real, the one who has attained realization knows that he will continue living, but will not be attached to anything, as he knows that all this is mere illusion.'

The last five verses, from thirty nine to forty four, enumerate the differences among Prakṛti, Puruṣa, and Brahmam.

3.28.39: 'It is obvious that a person is not his son or his riches. Similarly, Puruṣa or the Jīvātma is not the body it possesses.

3.28.40: 'Fire is different from the firewood, smoke or sparks; in the same way, Jīvātma is not the body.

3.28.41: 'Prakṛti from which the Bhūtās, the Indriyās, the intellect etc. are formed is not the Paramātma. The latter is the Brahmam or Pure Consciousness.

3.28.42: 'Ātma in the Bhūtās and the Bhūtās in the Ātma are reflections of each other.

3.28.43: 'Fire seems to be of different shapes and sizes depending on the firewood. Similarly, though the Jīvātma is one and the same, it appears to be different when it is residing in different forms or bodies in nature.

3.28.44: 'The Puruṣa or the Jīvātma of a devotee who has attained bhakti (devotion), jñāna (knowledge) and vairāgya (dispassion), overcomes the illusions seen in the Prakṛti and becomes one with Īśwara.

Here ends the twenty eighth chapter. In the next chapter, we see Devahūti asking more questions of her son Kapila.

3.29.1-5: 'You have explained to me the nature of Prakṛti, Puruṣa and Īśwara very well, as expounded in the Sāṁkhya Yoga. Now kindly tell me about the path of Bhakti Yoga. Please tell me how one can be dispassionate to the entire external world. Further, it is because of fear of time that people tend to do good karmas. So please tell me about 'time' as well, which is in fact one of the manifestations of God. Mankind is indeed fortunate that you have taken birth on Earth with the aim of lifting people out of the ocean of worldliness, where they are constantly moving up and down without knowing what to do. They are forever trapped in ignorance due to pride in their mortal bodies and as a result are unable to break the vicious circle of birth and death.'

3.29.6. This verse is spoken by Sage Maitreya. Addressing Vidura, he says that congratulating his mother on her thirst for the supreme knowledge, Bhagvān Kapila begins his response with great joy. Verses seven to forty five, i.e. all the remaining verses of this chapter, are spoken by the Lord.

3.29.7: 'Hé Mother! Bhakti Yoga, the path of devotion, varies from person to person, depending on the relative quanta of the Sātvik, Rājasik and Tāmasik qualities they possess.

3.29.8: 'The devotion of one who differentiates among others due to anger, deceit, unhealthy competition etc., who harms others, who wants to show others that he is a devotee and who wants to imitate other devotees is Tāmasik and hence undesirable.

3.29.9: 'The devotion of one who worships me in idol form while desiring fame, prosperity and materialistic pleasure is Rājasik. This is also not ideal as devotion is attached to desires.

3.29.10: 'One who worships God surrendering all karmās unto Him, and does so with the intent of reducing the evil effects of the sins committed by him has Sātvik devotion. Such devotion is acceptable.

3.29.11-12: 'Just like the Ganga flowing into the ocean ceaselessly, an ideal devotee is incorporated in me at all times. He has no sense of discrimination, believes in the unity of the universe and knows that it is the Supreme Being that resides in him as his soul also.

3.29.13-20: 'Such a devotee does not wish for or accept any of the five types of muktis namely 'sālokya mukti', i.e. living in the same place as the Lord, sārṣtya mukti', i.e. getting the same prosperity as the Lord, 'sāmīpya mukti', i.e. living near the Lord, 'sārūpya mukti', i.e. getting the same form as that of the Lord or 'sāyūjya mukti', i.e. becoming one with the Lord, even if I grant him any of these. This shows that he is beyond gunās and will become one with God upon his death. Thus, Bhakti Yoga is that with the help of which the three gunās can be conquered. By living a desireless, virtuous and admirable life, by practicing the peaceful Kriyā Yoga, by seeing, touching, glorifying, worshipping and saluting my idols, by experiencing me in all the bhūtās, by respecting the noble, by being kind to the deprived, by being friendly with equals, by shunning violent thoughts, words and actions, by chanting my name, by listening to spiritual discourses, by singing songs about me, by being in the company of devotees, by discarding ego, and by performing every act to make me happy, a man's mind is purified. Such a person who is engrossed in yoga without any distraction becomes one with his soul speedily, like how the wind takes any fragrance from its place of origin to peoples' nostrils with great speed.'

After describing the noblest form of Bhakti, the next six ślokās deal with the Tāmasik or the lowly form of Bhakti.

3.29.21-26: 'I exist in all the bhūtās at all times; this means I am everywhere. Not realizing this, some men worship me in idols. This is not real worship; it is in fact only pretence. Such worship will not bear any fruit. He who is proud of his body and sees others differently from himself without understanding that I am there in all bodies will never have peace of mind. I, whose idols are worshipped with a variety of offerings, will never be happy with those who hurt others. So idols should be worshipped earnestly until one sees me within him. Those who discriminate among other creations due to his own ego will always be scared of life in this world. Until the time he realizes that the Jīvātma in him and the Paramātma are one and the same, he will be afraid of death.

3.29.27: 'Therefore, knowing that I reside in everyone and everything, worship me with a sense of oneness in all creation, respecting superiors, being friendly with equals and helping those inferior to you.'

The next six ślokās are a comparative study of Jīvās at different levels.

3.29.28-33: 'Living beings are nobler than the non-living; and of the living, those who breathe are nobler. Of this category, those who have sense organs, along with intelligence, are higher in hierarchy than those with only intelligence. Of those which have sense organs, those which have the sense of taste are at a higher level than those which have the sense of touch only. Those which can make out smell also are at a still higher level. Those which can make out sound are higher than these, and still nobler are those which can see different forms. At a higher level are those with two rows of teeth. Among them, those with many feet are at a low level, those with four feet at an intermediate level and those with two feet like human beings at the highest. Of human beings, Brāhmins the noblest; yet among them, those who know the Vedās are nobler, and those who know the meanings of the Vedās also are the noblest. At a still higher level than those are the ones who can clear doubts of others. Along with all this, those who live righteously are noble. Among such people, those who are dispassionate are the noblest. At the highest level are those who do their duties without wishing for any reward. I do not see anyone at a higher hierarchy than one whose mind is fixed in me and does everything as a submission to me without a shred of arrogance, views the whole world equally as the place of my residence.

3.29.34: 'One should respect and salute the entire creation because God, the all controlling entity and the seat of all knowledge, has entered into it in the form of Jīvās.

3.29.35: 'Hé daughter of Manu! I have told you all about Sāṁkhya Yoga and Bhakti Yoga. By following any of these two paths itself, one who wishes to attain mokṣa can do so.'

After explaining Sāṁkhya Yoga and Bhakti Yoga, Bhagvān Kapila begins to describe in detail the nature of Time.

3.29.36-37: 'Nature of Time is the same as the nature of God. Time is the form of the Supreme Being. Prakṛti, Puruṣa, Indriyās etc. are all forms of God and also of Time. Time causes fear in those who see God separate from all these.

3.29.38-45: 'What enters into Bhūtās and gets them destroyed by the Bhūtās is Time. Everything happens as per Time. It has power over even the Devās who influence the whole universe. It is omnipresent and hence described as Viṣṇu, meaning 'existing everywhere'. For Time, there is neither a friend nor a foe. Forever alert, Time affects all those who are worldly. Those who know that Ātma is the only truth are not affected. It is due to fear of time that the wind blows, the sun glows, the clouds rain, and the stars twinkle. Trees and climbers and other plants produce flowers and fruits because of fear of Time. Rivers flow, oceans do not overflow, fire burns and the earth does not cave in by the weight of mountains as these are scared of Time. It is by following the rules of Time that the sky gives air to the creatures that breathe. Gods, who take pride in controlling the world comprising the living and the non-living, are also answerable to Time. Time is indivisible – it brings about the end, and comes without a beginning, but creates a beginning. Time creates people through people and kills destructive thieves through death.'

The last sentence of this chapter indicates that while the ignorant fear Time and die in fear, those who have attained the supreme knowledge and are liberated are not afraid of time, and become immortal.

The next chapter, i.e. chapter thirty three, comprises thirty four verses. All of them are spoken by the Lord.

3.30.1: 'People are affected by Time. However, just like clouds which are moved by wind do not know the power of the wind, people do not realize the supremacy of Time.

3.30.2: 'Whatever men accumulate for the sake of pleasure, with great difficulty, is destroyed by Time.

3.30.3: 'The ignorant think that houses, fields, riches and other such possessions of the body are permanent, only as they are a slave to desire.

3.30.4: 'In whichever form of life Jīvan is born, it craves for pleasure and not for dispassion.

3.30.5: 'Even those Jīvās that are residing in lowly forms of life and are leading a hellish life do not wish to leave their bodies as they are proud of their bodies and feel happy about their life.

3.30.6: 'Those who are born as human beings are full of ego and are proud that they have their own spouses, children, homes, vehicles, money, relations etc. in whom their minds are fixed.

3.30.7: 'Those who are worried about maintaining all this and are full of desires keep on committing errors.

3.30.8-9: 'Men who live under the influence of unfaithful women, enjoying the meaningless babble of infants, fall prey to senses. They feel that they are leading a happy life, even though they are living in their miserable homes. In reality, they are not happy.

3.30.10: 'Earning wealth through various methods by hurting others, they use this wealth in the upkeep of their family and themselves. Such people finally go to hell, with no family accompanying them.

3.30.11: 'People who are subject to greed turn to even others' wealth when their own businesses fail again and again.

3.30.12: 'Those who are inefficient in running their families, and work without getting any good result, who are unlucky and are without money, name, and common sense, are always lost in thought and sigh deeply in despair.

3.30.13: 'Family members of such a worthless man do not respect him, just like cruel farmers do not treat old and useless oxen well.

3.30.14-16: 'Even in such a miserable situation, this man who has not become dispassionate is controlled by those people whom he had controlled earlier. His body is now ugly due to wrinkles and he is waiting to die. He eats the food that is given to him without love or respect. He has many diseases and cannot eat much due to indigestion. His eyes protrude out because of the gas that tries to go out through his mouth. His respiratory tracts are blocked by phlegm due to which he cannot breathe properly. This results in a 'ghur ghur' sound coming out from his throat.

3.30.17-24: 'From all sides of this old man lying on his deathbed, his relatives call him out, but he does not reply. He who had been busy looking after his family till now, never trying to conquer his senses, dies a miserable death. It is one that is steeped in ignorance, with relatives crying all around. Just before death, he sees two ferocious looking messengers of Yama, the God of Death standing near him. Frightened beyond imagination, he urinates and defecates in bed. Transferring the dead man's Jīvan to his 'Yātanāśarīram' or body that bears pain, the messengers of Death tie him up with a rope around his neck and guide him along a lengthy path, like how a king's men guide a guilty man for punishment. On hearing their horrifying admonitions, he trembles in fear and begins to remember the wrong deeds he had done while alive. Hungry and thirsty, beaten with whips on the back, he walks along a hot desert. Falling down due to fatigue and getting up with difficulty, he somehow moves forward and finally reaches the abode of Yama, ninety nine thousand yojanās away in two or three muhūrtās.'

The next four verses are dedicated to a description of the dreadful sufferings of the Yātanāśarīram in hell.

3.30.25-28: 'Getting body parts burnt in scorching fire, having to eat their own body parts cut off by self or others, getting bitten by dogs, vultures, snakes, scorpions, and bees, limbs getting pulled apart by strong animals like elephants, being pushed down from mountains or suffocated under water or buried in pits etc., are some of the frightful experiences man or woman has to go through in the dark corridors of hell. These are the consequences of their own actions on Earth.'

The next six ślokās show that the lives of lower life forms are full of miseries and are equal to life in hell.

3.30.29-34: 'Hé Mother! Miseries similar to these are seen on the earth also. Lives of the lowly creatures are examples. A person who has lived for the sake of himself or for his family by hurting others ultimately gives up both, goes to the next world alone and faces the after effects of his sinful Karmās in hell. Like a man whose wealth has been stolen, he feels miserable in hell. He had committed many sins on Earth and has reached the darkness filled hell now. Until he has cleansed himself of his sins, he lives in the netherworld. After living the lives of lower animals, he is fully purified over time and then takes birth as a human being.'

The initial eleven ślokās of the next chapter, i.e. chapter thirty one, are a description of what happens from conception to the birth of a human baby.

3.31.1-11: 'Afterlife over, Jīvan enters the womb of a female through the sperm of the male. On the first day, it remains in liquid form, called 'kalalam'. In five days, it gradually becomes a global structure called 'budbudam'. By the tenth day, it gets the shape of an elliptical 'elandai' fruit. After that, it becomes a fleshy mass called 'peśi'. If the Jīvan has entered a female bird or any egg laying animal, this mass develops into an egg. In humans, head differentiates in a month. Limbs differentiate in two months and by the third month, nails, hair, bones, skin, and opening of the generative organ develop. By the fourth month, muscles and related structures differentiate. By the fifth month, the foetus starts experiencing hunger and thirst. In the sixth month, it gets surrounded by a delicate membrane called 'jarāyu' and begins to move within the womb. The foetus grows in size absorbing food and drinks consumed by the mother, and lies in unpleasant surroundings among tiny particles suspended in fluid and its own urine. Bearing the pain all over its delicate body caused by these particles, the foetus loses and regains its senses frequently. When the mother eats hot and spicy food also, the whole body of the foetus has to bear the pain. Enclosed within the 'jarāyu' and bound by the umbilical cord, the foetus remains in the womb in a sitting position with neck and back bent and head directed towards the chest. Like a caged bird, Jīvan remains inside the womb of the mother, and has no joy whatsoever. Keeping alive even without breathing, he recollects all the Karmās done in the previous lives, for by the seventh month, he has got consciousness. Inside the womb, the foetus keeps moving. Conscious of his body and realizing that the reason for this birth is his own past actions, the Jīvan prays to God with folded hands.'

The next ten verses, from twelve to twenty one, are spoken by the foetus, as related by Bhagvān Kapila. The foetus is referred to as 'jantu', meaning creature, right from the beginning. The 'jantu' says:

3.31.12-21: 'I, who had committed many crimes previously, offer my prayers at the lotus feet of that Lord who has attributed to me this place. The thought of Him destroys all fear in me. Māya has taken the form of Bhūtās, Indriyās and Antaḥkaraṇa, and this Māya has blurred my vision. This is why I had to bear the consequences of good and bad deeds. Sitting here, I pray to you, who are pure, who are without attributes, who possess the ultimate knowledge and who glisten in the hearts of grieving people. Even though I live in a body made of Pancabhūtās, my true reality is hidden from me, but you are not hidden so. You are independent of everything and Prakṛti and Puruṣa act as per your instructions. I worship you, who are such a God. I am now able to realize that human beings are born and die due their own Karmās. This has been possible only because of your blessing. I seek refuge in you, oh Lord. We are bound to follow the path of Karmās, but you are free and are present in all the movable and immovable entities of the universe. We worship you to get a release from this binding. This Jīvan is living in absolute misery now in a cavity inside another individual, containing blood and urine, and being burnt in the fire of hunger. All the time I am calculating for how many more months I will have to stay here. I am in great sorrow! Hé Lord, when will I be sent out? I am ten months old now. You have been magnanimous enough to let me have this ultimate realization. How can I express my gratitude to you? I can only fold my hands in worship. I, made of the seven types of body tissues, can see with the help of my intellect that this body will have to go through joys and sorrows. I can also see you, the indestructible and omnipresent Supreme Being, with neither a beginning nor an end. Such a realization is possible for only a human being. On second thoughts, though I prayed for release from this womb, I now remember that once out in the senseless world, I shall forget the truth about you, will be a victim of your Māya, have pride in my body and be part of the vicious circle of death and birth. Therefore, oh Lord, kindly let it be that sitting here, I meditate upon your lotus feet, thereby freeing myself from the misery of repeated cycles of birth in the form of various creatures and subsequent death. In this way, I can come out of the darkness of ignorance and raise myself rapidly to a sorrow-less state.'

After relating this prayer by the foetus within the mother's womb, Bhagvān Kapila continues:

3.31.22: 'The foetus in the mother's womb is thus an intelligent being. Knowing the ultimate truth, he praises the Supreme Lord. By now he is ten months old. The air inside the womb is pushing him in such a way that he is in an inverted position.

3.31.23: 'During delivery, he is suddenly pushed out. The anguish experienced at this time leads to the foetus losing his consciousness. Therefore, all his earlier contemplations are wiped out. He comes out with great difficulty.

3.31.24: 'He falls onto a surface covered in blood and moves his limbs like a lowly reptile. The divine knowledge is gone. He cries out loudly.

3.31.25: 'Those who take care of him are not able to understand what he wants; thus many times, he gets what he does not want. He is unable to express his needs.

3.31.26: 'Lying down wherever he is laid down, he cannot even scratch himself whenever he feels itchy. He cannot sit or get up from his place and thus cries loudly.

3.31.27: 'He has lost all memories of God and is crying frequently. When his delicate skin is injured by insect bites, he cries out loudly, like a big worm bitten by several smaller ones.

3.31.28-29: 'In this way, infancy gets over, and then childhood begins. Having had to bear with various types of miseries as an infant and later as a child, the person becomes a youth. Due to ignorance, he craves for many things and on not getting them, becomes sad and agitated and fights with those who do not fulfill his desires.

3.31.30: 'The ignorant Jīvan is not aware of the fact that the mortal body is made of the five Bhūtās. He is full of ego; his mind is filled by the thoughts of 'I, my and mine'.

3.31.31-32: 'Whichever Jīvan, due to ignorance, does deeds that give grief, is born in the material world, and has to face the consequences of his deeds. If he continues performing wrongful deeds in the company of other ignorant ones, he will have to go to hell after death.

3.31.33-35: 'Honesty, cleanliness, kindness, frugality in speech, capability of differentiating between good and bad, prosperity, shame on doing wrong deeds, power of endurance, ability to control senses, devotion to God – all these good qualities are lost if a man with these qualities keeps the company of those whose minds are forever turbulent, ignorant and wicked, just like a man who falls a prey to lust on associating with women. Therefore, do not get into the company of the ignorant, wicked people.

3.31.36-42: 'Lord Brahma the Creator was attracted to his own daughter Goddess Saraswati. Realizing this, she took the form of a doe and ran. Lord Brahma immediately took the form of a deer and ran after her. It is really difficult not to get attracted by women. Of all who were created by Brahma and those created by Brahma's creations, except Rishi Nārāyaṇa, an incarnation of mine, who else is there capable of overcoming the temptation offered by women, who are in reality, manifestations of Māya, my own feminine form? Therefore, men who wish to reach the other shore of yoga, by virtue of good company, should never be attracted by women. They must realize that women, created by God in the form of Māya, are like wells hidden by tall grass, leading to their downfall.

'In the same way, women who accept men, my own Māya in the male form, as husbands for providing wealth, offspring and homes, are waylaid. Women who wish for mokṣa must realize that attraction to men is an obstacle in their path as these men were women in their previous births and had distracted men themselves.

3.31.43-48: 'Jīvās travel from one loka to another and do karmās incessantly in their bodies. The presence of gross bodies comprised of Pancabhūtās, Indriyās and mind is the obstacle in Jīvās' attaining mokṣa. When the Jīvās realize that they are only witnesses to everything experienced by their gross bodies, they shed their ego. For example, when a person's eyes lose the power to see, we say that his sense organ for seeing is no more functional. Similar is the case with the other sense organs. In such situations, one must not lose courage. He should know that destruction happens only to the gross body. He should apply his intelligence. Dedicating his body to this world of illusion, he should move on till the body falls. He should understand that even after body falls, Jīvan remains and enters into another body later on. One who has known this truth through contemplation is never afraid of anything, not even death.'

The next chapter, which is chapter thirty two, comprises forty three ślokās – all of which are spoken by Bhagvān Kapila.

3.32.1-4: 'The man who lives in his house performing his household duties continues doing the same and obtains as a result materialistic pleasures like wealth. In this way, immersed in desires, he is not able to use his power of discrimination and hence is indifferent to the Supreme Being. He performs yāgās and worships various Gods and spirits of his dead ancestors with great devotion. Such a person who has profound faith in Devās and spirits goes to the world of the Moon after death, enjoys godly life by drinking amṛt and relishing other such pleasures, after which he finally returns to the world of the humans. When Bhagvān Viṣnu lies down on Ādiśeṣa for yogic sleep, then the worlds attainable by householders are also destroyed.

3.32.5-7: 'The intelligent, who are not interested in materialistic pleasures, who perform their karmās as a dedication to God, who have controlled their minds, who are not egoistic and who do not do anything with the intention of achieving sensual pleasures, travel through the world of the sun after discarding their mortal bodies, and attain Īśwara, who is responsible for creation, sustenance and dissolution of the universe, who is the controller of Prakṛti, and who is present everywhere, on account of their sātvik nature and pure antaḥkaraṇa.

3.32.8-10: 'Those who worship Lord Brahma as the supreme God reach the Brahma Loka after death and live there joyfully till the time of Brahma Pralaya, which occurs after every Dwiparārdha or two Parārdhās, which is the life span of the Creator, when he becomes one with Mahāviṣnu. (One Parārdha is one crore crore human days.) Brahma Pralaya begins when Lord Brahma, proud of the universe encompassing the three gunās and characterized by the earth, water, fire, air, sky, mind, indriyās, subjects like sound, ego etc., decides to put an end to it. Those yogis, who have reached the Brahma Loka after death and are enjoying life there, ultimately conquer their minds, give up all desires and get unified with Lord Viṣnu along with the Creator.

3.32.11: 'Therefore, Oh pure one with wholesome love, seek refuge in the Supreme Being who resides within the hearts of everyone and whose greatness is well known.

3.32.12-14: 'Even Lord Brahma, who is the Creator of all the living and the non-living, takes birth again as Brahma after the end of his life span, not going to any higher level as he takes credit for his work of creation and becomes egoistic.

3.32.15: 'Those who had enjoyed the prosperities of Brahma Loka due to their good deeds also return to this world of humans when creation starts anew due to revival of the three gunās.

3.32.16-22: 'Those who are full of desires, yet perform all karmās dutifully and those who are not able to control their senses, with minds never still due to their strong rājasik nature, yet worship their ancestors sincerely every day and those who are more interested in listening to corrupt worldly stories than the stories of the Supreme Lord who can help them cross the ocean of life effortlessly – such people are bound by their past karmās. After death, they reach the Pitṛ Loka. Hé pure one! When the good life in the Pitṛ Loka ends, the Devās in charge send them back to this world. They are thus born again in the Manuṣya Loka. This cycle is repeated endlessly. Therefore Oh Mother, have complete faith in the Supreme Being and worship Him wholeheartedly.

3.32.23-26: 'When devotion to the Supreme God who dwells everywhere becomes stronger and stronger, dispassion towards this materialistic world and true enlightenment will follow automatically. The external stimuli are all equivalent, yet the mind because of its union with the indriyās experiences some stimuli as good and others as bad. For example, one likes some sounds and not some others. When this differentiation blurs and he experiences everything equally, he attains the supreme knowledge. This ultimate knowledge is the manifestation of the Paramātma, also described as Brahmam, Īśwara, Bhagvān or Puruṣa. It is all one and the same.

3.32.27-31: 'What yogis achieve through different types of yoga is one and the same – detachment from everything and everyone. The sense of plurality is an illusion created by the sense organs. On the dissolution of this illusion, knowledge shines by itself. The Supreme Being is seen as different parts and aspects of the universe and seems to be plural, though singular in reality. One who practices yoga with dedication has devotion and a controlled mind, and is dispassionate to worldly objects. He realizes this truth. Hé respected mother! I have expounded to you this knowledge in detail. By understanding this in its entirety, you can envisage the true nature of Prakṛti and Puruṣa.

3.32.32: 'The end result of Jñānayoga, based on non-existence of gunās and ending in me, and Bhaktiyoga, whose indication is pure and undiluted devotion, is one and the same – both lead to God-realization.

3.32.33: 'One and the same thing is perceived in different ways by different sense organs based on the stimuli they create like sight, smell, taste etc. It is exactly like this that one and the same Supreme Being is perceived in different ways by different interpreters.

3.32.34-36: 'Union with the Supreme Being, who is beyond all gunās and who is self-luminescent, can be accomplished by various means like yāgās, good acts beneficial to others, penance, learning the Vedās, introspection, conquering the senses, dedicating all acts to God, yoga, undiluted devotion to God, righteousness, and dispassion.

3.32.37-40: 'I have told you in great detail about the four aspects of Bhaktiyoga and the true nature of Time which enters all the living and the non-living and works silently. I have also told you about the Jīvātmās which remain ignorant about their own nature due to the egoism of the bodies they reside in. Do not impart this knowledge in Sāṁkhya Śāstrā to the cruel who distress others, the arrogant, those who pretend to be ethical, those who are attracted to worldly pleasures, who are not my devotees and who are in contradiction with my devotees.

3.32.41-42: 'On the other hand, this knowledge can be imparted to those who listen attentively to what is spoken, have faith in the speaker, are humble and not jealous of others, are not of a fault finding nature, along with those who are kind to all creatures, who are interested in knowing the truth, who are uninterested in sensual joys, have a mind capable of introspection, are happy to see the growth of others and love me above everyone and everything else.

3.32.43: 'Hé Mother! Whoever with his mind fixed in me listens to or praises this discourse will definitely reach me.'

Kapilagīta ends here.

The first verse of chapter thirty three is spoken by Sage Maitreya to Vidura.

3.33.1: 'Listening to these invaluable pieces of advice of her son Bhagvān Kapila, Devahūti became enlightened. Prostrating before him, now her preceptor, she sang his glory.'

3.33.2-8: These seven ślokās are sung by Devahūti. She says that the same Lord, whose capability is infinite and who has an immense power of imagination, creates, sustains and destroys everything. At the same time, He is not involved in anything. She wonders how the Supreme Lord, within whom the entire universe exists, who lay on a Peepal leaf sucking his toe during the great deluge, took the form of a baby in her womb. As if in response to her own query, she says the Supreme Lord takes birth in different forms at different times for the benefit of mankind, and her son is no exception. She expresses her absolute joy and deepest gratitude to God as she has been fortunate enough to see Him in person. Finally, she prostrates before her son, Bhagvān Kapila, who she says is famed as Viṣṇu in the Purāṇās and the Paramapuruṣa in the Sāṁkhya Śāstrās. By meditating on Him, she is sure that dispassionate devotees can become enlightened and attain permanent liberation from the materialistic world.

3.33.9: Sage Maitreya says that on being praised by his mother thus, Bhagvān Kapila, displaying his deep affection to his mother, speaks to her in a voice broken by affection.

3.33.10-11: 'Oh Mother, by following the principles elucidated by me, which you can easily follow, you will surely attain mokṣa without delay. Previously also, the enlightened have described Brahman as such. I have elaborated the same principle. Those who listen to this discourse and understand it will attain me.'

3.33.12: Thus, describing to his mother in great detail the

truth about Brahman, and feeling assured that she has gained Brahmajñāna in the right sense, a fully gratified Kapila takes her permission and leaves the place.

3.33.13: In this verse, Maitreya says that Devahūti remained in her hermitage, following her son's advice and conquering her senses and mind, and got immersed in severe penance.

Further, he elaborates how Devahūti attains mokṣa at the end of her penance.

3.33.37: In this last verse, Sage Maitreya declares that the mind of anyone who reads or listens to the Kapilagīta will become calm. Fixed in the thought of God, he will become one with God at the end of his earthly life.

CHAPTER 2

RUDRAGĪTA

As mentioned earlier, the third and fourth cantos of Śrīmad Bhāgavatam are presented in the form of a dialogue between Sage Maitreya and the learned Vidura, uncle to the Pāṇdavās and Kaurāvās. Rudragīta is part of the fourth canto. This canto comprises thirty one chapters. Of these, from chapter twenty four onwards till the end, the story of the ten brothers called Pracetas brothers is narrated in detail. In the first few verses, a short account is given about the ancestors of the brothers, starting with King Pṛthu.

King Pṛthu was a descendant of Dhruva, grandson of the first man Manu. He made his country more prosperous than ever before. He also brought about many reforms in his country and performed many sacrifices for the spiritual upliftment of his people. In fact, the Earth is known as Pṛthvi, meaning daughter of Pṛthu, in Sanskrit, Hindi and many other Indian languages. After serving his people tirelessly by all means, King Pṛthu went away to the forest for penance and in due course of time attained mokṣa. After Pṛthu, his son Vijitāśwa became king. He was followed by Havirdhāna and then Barhiṣat.

King Barhiṣat was a lover of yagyās. He performed so many

yagyās of different types in so many different places that people started calling him Prācīna Barhiss, meaning one who laid down barhiss (darbha grass) with tips towards prācī (the east). (Darbha or dūrwa is the common lawn grass that is used in pūjās).

He fathered ten sons, all of whom were equally virtuous and had the same name – Pracetass. When the brothers came of age, their father told them to take their lineage forward. The Pracetass brothers believed that without the blessings of the Supreme Being, nothing good would happen in the world. So they left the palace in search of a suitable place for penance. On the way, they saw a beautiful large lake with lotus blooms, swans and colourful fishes. Bees buzzed on the lotus flowers and birds chirped happily in the vicinity. Gandharvās and Kinnarās sang melodiously. As the brothers stood watching and listening all these, they saw the elegant form of Lord Rudra, i.e. Śiva, emerging from the lake.

At this point of the story, Vidura asked Maitreya: "It is not easy for anyone to have the darśan of Parameśwara so effortlessly. So how did the Pracetass brothers achieve that?"

Sage Maitreya then explained to Vidura that Lord Śiva was pleased with the absolute devotion of the brothers. This was why he decided to bless them. A perfect guru had found ten perfect śiṣyās. The sage then continued the story.

Śiva told the princes, "Meditate on Nārāyana. He is the Supreme Being. I shall teach you some verses in His praise. Sing them with devotion."

These verses together make the Rudragīta or Rudragītam. Before the beginning of this Gītam, Śrī Mahādeva spoke to the Pracetas brothers thus:

4.24.27: 'I have appeared before you because you are the sons of Prācīna Barhiss and are desirous of worshipping God. My blessing will be with you for the successful completion of your efforts.

4.24.28: 'I like those who are unattached to the results of their actions and who worship the Supreme Being with total devotion.

4.24.29: 'Those who lead a virtuous life based on dharma

attain Brahmaloka after a hundred births. People better placed than them attain me. However, true devotees of Lord Vāsudeva, like various devas and me, directly reach Vaikunṭha on the dissolution of their physical bodies.

4.24.30: 'As you are devotees of Vāsudeva, you are dear to me, like him. Similarly, devotees of Vāsudeva like me too.

4.24.31: 'The Gīta that I am about to teach you is holy, enjoyable and capable of giving one mokṣa. This should be chanted with clarity. I shall recite these verses now. Listen well.'

As stated earlier, the third and the fourth cantos of the Bhāgavat Purān is a dialogue between sage Maitreya and Vidura. Thus, Verse 32 comprises the words of Sage Maitreya.

4.24.32: "Srī Rudra, with a heart full of devotion to Lord Nārāyana and kindness to the princes who were standing with folded hands, addressed them."

Verses 33 to 68 of Chapter 24, Canto 4, of the Bhāgavat Purāna comprise the Rudragīta. These are the ślokās Sri Rudra taught the Pracetass brothers to be chanted for ultimate liberation.

24.24.33: 'You shower benediction on the enlightened who have realised the truth about the soul. Kindly grant me the same too. Salutations to you, Oh omnipresent Bhagvān.

4.24.34: 'Salutations to you, Nārāyaṇa, from whose navel arose the lotus of creation, and who is the power intrinsic in the five elememts (panca-bhūtās), the five senses (panca-tanmātrās), and the five sense organs (pancendriyās). Salutations to you, Vāsudeva, the one who is ever peaceful, who is above all emotions and is self-luminescent.

4.24.35: 'Salutations to Sankarṣana (Ādiśeṣa) who is immortal and subtle, and Pradyumna, who is the innermost soul and the manifestation of intellect and consciousness.

4.24.36: 'Salutations to Anirudha, who is the god of senses and sense organs. Salutations at all times to the Sun God, who is complete in himself, who is ever perpetual without any increase or decrease in size, who is present in the inner being of all creatures, who leads the way to heaven and liberation.

4.24.37: 'Salutations to the God of Fire, whose flames are golden, and who makes vedik rites possible, and the Moon God who provides food to the gods and the souls of our ancestors and who promotes the growth of plants used in vedik sacrifices.

4.24.38: 'Salutations to the Supreme Lord in the form of Water, who quenches the thirst of all living beings. Salutations to the Supreme Being in the form of the Earth, of whom the bodies of all living beings are made.

4.24.39: 'Salutations to the Supreme Lord who, in the form of Air, protects the three worlds and who is the power of the mind, sense organs and body; to the Sky who is present inside and outside, and because of whom all things get to be known.

4.24.40: 'Salutations to Heaven (Swargaloka) which is attainable through virtuous deeds, to Karma itself, which motivates one to actions and also inertia or tranquillity, and to the souls of our ancestors.

4.24.41: 'Salutations to the God of Death, who gives agony, which is the result of sinful acts of living beings. Salutations to you, oh God of all the gods, who knows the wishes of all, and who can fulfil all those wishes.

4.24.42: 'Salutations to the noble Dharma, i.e. righteousness or morality; to Śrī Kṛṣna, personification of everlasting knowledge; to Purāṇapuruṣa, i.e. the oldest possible entity; to the Supreme God who spread the message of Sāṁkhya Yoga.

4.24.43: 'Salutations to the Lord who represents the three supreme powers and ego, i.e. Śrī Rudra; to the God of Knowledge; and to the God of Speech.

4.24.44: 'Kindly appear before us, who, like all your devotees, wish passionately to see you. Kindly show us your divine form which is your worshippers' object of ultimate love and gives intense happiness to all our sense organs at the same time.

4.24.45: 'Your form is as soft as a rain cloud and your complexion is dark, possessing an all inclusive beauty; your four hands are long, graceful and magnificent and your face is round and charming.

4.24.46: 'Your eyes shaped like lotus petals, your arched eyebrows, beautiful nose, glowing teeth, shining cheeks and perfect ears adorn your countenance.

4.24.47: 'Your eyes smile with love for your devotees, your forehead looks beautified with short curls of hair, your attire is yellow, like the pollen grains of lotus flowers and the jewels on your ears are radiant.

4.24.48: 'Your crown, bangles, necklaces, anklets, waist chain, pendent and the Kaustubha gem glow brightly. You are wearing a beautiful floral garland and you carry a conch, discus, mace, and a lotus in your four hands.

4.24.49: 'Your shapely neck is like that of a lion. Via the Kaustubha gem that shines on that neck, Goddess Lakṣmi resides permanently on your chest.

4.24.50: 'The folds on your banyan leaf shaped narrow abdomen keep quivering when you inhale and exhale, while the deep navel on your stomach looks as if it is ready to absorb the world inward.

4.24.51: 'On the yellow silk cloth around your dark waist, shines the waist chain of gold. Below that, your thighs, knees, ankles, and feet are exceptionally good-looking and all these give extreme joy to the mind.

4.24.52: 'Oh Master! With the moon-light like glow of your toe nails, please remove the darkness of ignorance in our minds. Even to the ignorant who worship your feet, shining brightly like lotus flowers bloomed in spring, you show the right path, destroying all their fear. Please show us this attractive form of yours.

4.24.53: 'Such a form deserves to be worshipped and meditated upon by devotees who wish to make their conscience pure, because devotion to God protects the righteous.

4.24.54: 'Though common men cannot attain you, true devotees can. You are attainable to those who are enlightened. You are worshipped by all the wise people and those who live in heaven.

4.24.55: 'It is difficult even for the virtuous to attain you by worship, after giving up all desires. Yet no enlightened person will wish to be one with nothing other than your divine feet.

4.24.56: 'The God of Death, who is capable of destroying the whole world by a mere movement of his eyebrows, knows very well that he can never approach one who has sought refuge in you.

4.24.57: 'Even the company of people who have taken total refuge in you is highly beneficial. The company of such people, even for a short while, is not equal to heaven or liberation, what to say of the pleasures one can get in this material world.

4.24.58: 'Please let us have the company of those whose sins have been washed away by your feet, those who have destroyed their sins by taking bath in the holy rivers of your fame and those who are virtuous by nature and kind to all that is created. Kindly bless us to be in such company.

4.24.59: 'When a devotee is blessed and his mind becomes pure, when his mind does not become confused and fall into the depths of ignorance, then that saintly person understands your truth and gets the vision of your true self.

4.24.60: 'You are that intrinsic power in which the universe is manifested and which manifests in the universe. You are the potency shining throughout the universe and, like the atmosphere, permeate everyone and everything on both the inside and the outside.

4.24.61: 'We realize that you are that Supreme Being. With your infinite power of illusion, you create, maintain, and destroy this universe again and again. You remain emotionless as Māya is not capable of evoking any response in you. At the same time, ordinary men, as they are subject to the working of Māya, believe that the universe is real.

4.24.62: 'Those enlightened yogis realise the fact that as the five elements, the five sense organs and the mind work because you motivate them to do so, and that you are present everywhere. Knowing you thus to be the supreme energy, they worship you.

4.24.63: 'In the beginning, only you existed. Māya, the Power of Illusion, was dissolved in you. Later, the three Guṇās, namely Satvaṁ, Rajas and Tamas, ingrained in Māya, got separated from one another. As a result of this, the Universe comprising Mahattatva (total material energy), Ahaṁkāra (ego), Pancabhūta (the five elements of sky, air, fire, water and earth), Devās, Ṛṣis, living creatures etc., came into being.

4.24.64: 'In the physical bodies of the living beings, you entered as Soul (antarātma). The mortal body, under the influence of Jīvan (Life force), keeps enjoying momentary pleasures through sense organs, like bees collect and consume honey. However, the Antarātma existing within bodies is immortal. Only the wise are aware of this truth.

4.24.65: 'In the form of Time, you manage the elements with the elements themselves. Like a powerful storm disseminating clouds, you distribute the five elements in the universe. The enlightened know this phenomenon to be a fact.

4.24.66: 'The ignorant are always after pleasures ensuing from enjoyment through sense organs and believe that what they are doing is right. Such people spend their life in the foolish pursuit of materialistic desires. In the meantime, like a hungry snake crawling after a rat, you approach them unexpectedly in the form of death.

4.24.67: 'Which wise men, who are aware of this fact, will give up your lotus feet? Our precept worships you. The fourteen Manus do the same by convention, though without the same resolve.

4.24.68: 'Hé Supreme Lord! You are the universal soul. We, who know that the whole world is subject to devastation by Time, are taking refuge in you, the protector of all. This will remove all our fears.'

Here ends Rudragītam. Thereafter, in eleven verses (4.24.69-79), Sri Rudra advises the Pracetas brothers how to chant this divine song for maximal benefit.

4.24.69: 'Hé Princes! Remove all defects like anger from your mind, remain healthy by living life in the right manner, concentrate on God and chant these verses continuously. Everything auspicious will happen to you.

4.24.70: 'Worship Sri Hari, praise Him and meditate on Him, who is present in you and also in all things movable and immovable.

4.24.71: 'Receiving this 'Yogādeś' from me, recite this song with full attentiveness while living like sages, following all the rules applicable to them.

4.24.72: 'Advice in the form of this song was given by Lord Brahma to his sons, including Maharṣi Bhṛgu and me, for the purpose of helping him in Creation.

4.24.73: 'All of us who learnt these verses and chanted them properly were able to fulfil our wish which was creation of different species.

4.24.74: 'Therefore, one who chants these verses incessantly with a firm resolve, fixing his mind steadfastly in Vāsudeva with a feeling of surrender unto Him, will attain happiness and prosperity without delay.

4.24.75: 'Of all praiseworthy achievements, Jnānam (Knowledge) is the noblest. One who takes the help of the ship of Jnānam can cross the vast ocean of sorrow with ease.

4.24.76: 'By learning and chanting this Gītam sung by me with devotion, one can worship the Supreme Lord, who is difficult to worship.

4.24.77: 'Single minded and patient chanting of these verses will please the Lord very much. He, who is the ultimate refuge of everyone, will grant such a person all his wishes.

4.24.78: 'One who gets up early in the morning, cleanses his body, joins his hands, and sings or listens to this stotram sincerely will be freed of bondage due to karmas.

4.24.79: 'Hé Princes! This Gītaṁ, advised to you by me, is about the Supreme Lord, who is all-knowing. Do penance unto Him, chanting this Gītaṁ with undivided attention. In the end, at the right time, you will get from Him all you want.'

Here ends chapter twenty four. The first few ślokās of chapter twenty five of canto four depict what Sage Maitreya says to Vidura.

4.25.1: 'When Lord Śiva, the personification of jñānam, concluded his advice thus, the Pracetas brothers bowed before him and paid obeisance to him. While they were still looking at his divine form, Lord Śiva vanished from their view.

4.25.2: The Pracetas brothers did penance, standing in water and chanting Rudragītam, for many years.

In the end, they got Lord Mahāviṣnu's darśan and received His blessings. As per the directive of the Lord, they married Māruṣi, the daughter of the tree goddess and returned to the palace. Dakṣa was their son, through whom the lineage was continued.

The Pracetass brothers ruled the land for long. Gradually, they lost all interest in life. They had done their duty admirably. They now desired mokṣa, and hence travelled westward and reached the seashore.

There they met Sage Nārada. The brothers told him: 'Lord Śiva, and later Śrī Hari, had explained the supreme truth to us. We had understood it too at that time. Later, as we were engaged in worldly acts, we forgot most of it. Please enlighten us now.'

Sage Nārada then explained to them many vedāntic truths. Finally, he stated the glory of Lord Viṣnu thus: 'Water need be poured only at the base of a tree, but all the parts get water. Thus, it is not necessary to water the branches, leaves, flowers and fruits separately. Moreover, it is also not possible to do so. Similarly, food and water consumed through the mouth reach the whole body. In the same way, there is no need to please all the Devās; it is not possible either. Please Śrī Hari and all other Devās will be pleased in turn.'

Blessing the Pracetas brothers, Sage Nārada left for Brahmaloka. Later, the brothers meditated on Lord Nārāyana as instructed by the sage and became one with God.

CHAPTER 3

YAMAGĪTA

In the seventh canto of Śrīmad Bhāgavatam, we see King Parīkṣit asking Maharṣi Śuka how it is that Bhagvān Viṣṇu, to whom all are equal, ends up killing some people, most of them Asurās.

Śuka Brahmarṣi was happy to hear this question. He decided to explain the matter to the king citing an incident which had taken place after the Rājasūya Yajña performed by Rāja Yudhiṣṭhira. There, Lord Kṛṣṇa had cut off wicked Śiśupāla's head with his Sudarśana Cakra. Immediately after the death of Śiśupāla, a glowing light had emanated from his body and merged in Kṛṣṇa. Seeing this mystical occurrence, Yudhiṣṭhira had asked Sage Nārada, who was present there to witness the Yajña, how the evil-minded Śiśupāla could achieve this feat, impossible even for the pious.

The answer that Sage Nārada gave to Raja Yudhiṣṭhira in that assembly, in presence of the spectators, is being narrated here by Maharṣi Śuka to King Parīkṣit. Sage Nārada said that Bhagvān is never affected by flattery or scorn, anger or love, devotion or fear. These features affect only those who give importance to the body and mind. That is why Bhagvān does not mind being thought of with any of these emotions. Those who constantly think of the

Lord with animosity are also remembering him relentlessly. This is enough to wash their sins away. Śiśupāla and Dantavaktra are the third and final births of Jaya and Vijaya, the gate-keepers of Mahāviṣṇu, after the duos of Hiraṇyākṣa and Hiranyakaśipu, and Rāvaṇa and Kumbhakarṇa. The gate-keepers had been cursed by the Ṛṣis Sanaka and his brothers to be born on Earth three times as evil men or Rākṣasās. All six held Viṣṇu with vengeance and loathing; all were killed by the Lord and given Mokṣa.

Those who consider the body as all important are ignorant. Such people become sad at the death of others. The truth is that grieving for the dead is meaningless as it is only the body that dies.

To prove his point, Sage Nārada tells Yudhiṣṭhira an incident. When Hiraṇyakaśipu came to know of the death of his brother Hiraṇyākṣa at the hands of Mahāviṣṇu, he was very sad and also furious at the Lord. At his command, his servants immediately got engaged in heinous crimes against all the good people in the country to spite Viṣṇu. At the same time, he also consoled his mother and the dead brother's wife and sons. He told them that the Ātma remains immortal even after death of the body. As such, they should not grieve over Hiraṇyākṣa's death.

In validation of his statement, Hiraṇyakaśipu narrated to them the story of a king by the name of Suyajña of the kingdom of Uśīnaram. One day, the king was killed in a war. His queens and the others had gathered around his dead body lying on the battlefield. The queens wept loudly, praising the king for his various virtues and blaming the gods for the cruel fate handed out to the good king. Unable to bear their grief, they wanted to die with their husband. They lay down on the ground, hugging him, thereby preventing the king's cremation.

At this point, Yama, the God of Death, appeared on the scene, in the form of a small boy. All that the boy tells the inconsolable relations of King Suyajña is known as the Yamagīta, covering twenty one ślokās.

In the form of the boy, Yama said:

7. 2.37: 'These people are quite elderly, and know the ways

of life; yet it is strange that they are so ignorant. It is very sad indeed that despite knowing that man has to go back to where he has come from, they are grieving over his death.

7.2.38: 'We are children, brought to this world and left here. Yet we are not afraid. We are not troubled by anyone in this world for we are protected by the same force that protected us in our mother's womb.

7.2.39: 'Hé dear women, know that it is God who created this world, is sustaining it and will destroy it when the time comes. The whole universe is his toy. Only he has the power to reward us or punish us.

7.2.40: 'A thing which has fallen on the public road will remain safe, if it is guarded by him. Yet something which is kept safely inside the house will be destroyed, if it is not protected by him. Similarly, an orphan living alone in the forest, if under his shelter, lives well. At the same time, one who is secure within his house is killed if he is not protected by God.

7.2.41: 'Living things are born at fixed times, based on their own Karmās, and die at fixed times. Though the Ātma is present in the body, it does not acquire any guṇa of the body.

7.2.42: 'The body of a person is not he; he believes so due to ignorance. The real 'he' is the Ātma.

It is just like a house owner not being the house itself. Bubbles seen on water are not water; they soon disappear. Similarly, all living creatures die sooner or later.

7.2.43: 'Fire is not firewood, though it is there in firewood. It manifests externally only when the firewood is lit. There is air in the body; but it becomes apparent only when we breathe. The sky is there everywhere, but it does not merge with anything. The Ātma in the body thus remains a separate entity.

7.2.44: 'Oh foolish women, see, the one for whom you are grieving is lying down here. Can he answer your queries now? Did he ever do so while he was living also? The one who responded to you was only his body.

7.2.45: 'Even when he was alive, you have seen only his deha, i.e. his physical body. It was his sense organs that reacted to your word or actions, not the Prāṇa, i.e. the life breath in him. You have seen neither his Prāṇa nor his Ātma.

7.2.46: 'Ātma is omnipresent. It receives high or lowly bodies made of the elements, sense organs and mind. Later, by its own decision, it leaves the body. It is not the deha nor is it the Prāṇa.

7.2.47: 'As long as a body has Prāṇa, it is alive. A person is proud of his body only till there is Prāṇa in it. The connection with Karmās, the joys and sorrows originating from it and the link with Māya exists only until the body is alive.

7.2.48: 'Thinking that the Guṇās are real is a myth, like a dream. Things which can be experienced through sense organs are all unreal.

7.2.49: 'Therefore, those who know what is permanent and what is not, do not grieve in this world. By grieving, the mortal nature of the body cannot be changed. It is therefore useless to grieve. The soul is anyway immortal, so there is no need to mourn for the soul too.

7.2.50: 'Once a hunter, designated by God as Antaka (Spirit of Death) of birds, went to a forest and spread his net on the ground, with some grains scattered in it.

7.2.51: 'A pair of Kulinga (Plover) birds were flying about in the forest. The she Kulinga got trapped in the net.

7.2.52: 'Despite trying her best, she could not get out. Seeing this, her mate became extremely sad. In his anguish, the he Kulinga cried out loudly, accusing the God of Death for his cruelty.

7.2.53: 'The male bird lamented, 'Oh unkind God! You are capable of doing anything and everything. My wife deserves kindness. Of what use is she to the God of Death?

7.2.54: 'I have to spend the rest of my life in utter grief without her. Of what use is such a life to me? Let the God of Death take away this half-body of mine too.

7.2.55: 'My young chicks, who have not grown wings yet, are without a mother now. How will I take care of them? My unfortunate chicks will be waiting for their mother.'

7.2.56: 'In this way, the father bird wailed loudly. On hearing this wail, the hunter who was hiding a little distance away shot an arrow from afar and killed him.

7.2.56: 'So do not be foolish like this bird. Even if you weep for a hundred years, you are not going to get your husband back.'

Hiraṇyakaśipu thus concluded the story.

7.2.58: 'All the dead king's kin were astounded by this speech of the boy. They understood that all that was seen around them were mortal.

7.2.59: 'Concluding his address, the boy left the scene. The relatives then performed the last rites of King Suyajña as per customs.

7.2.60: 'It is only the ignorant who are confused about who the Ātma is and who others are. Only they will weep on the death of others. The truth is that only Brahmam is real and everything else is illusory. The wise do not grieve for themselves or others.'

Narrating this story, Sage Nārada concludes:

7.2.61: 'Listening to Hiraṇyakaśipu, his brother Hiraṇyākṣa's wife, and the two brothers' mother Diti stopped lamenting. They concluded that nothing existed other than Brahman and thus let this ultimate truth sink fully in their minds.'

The second chapter of the seventh canto ends here.

CHAPTER 4

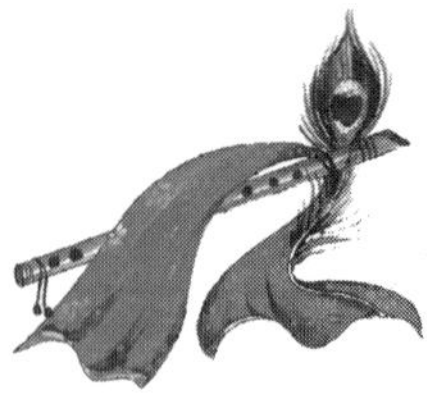

VEṆUGĪTA

The tenth canto of Śrīmad Bhāgavatam, as mentioned earlier, describes in detail the birth of Kṛṣṇa and his exploits. Though born in Mathura as the the son of Vasudeva and Devaki, he was brought up in Gokul, and later, Vṛndāvan, by Nandagopa and Yaśoda. The incarnation of the Supreme Lord Mahāviṣṇu, this divine child was the darling of the people. He had sent to Yamaloka many Asurās in his infancy and early childhood. With elder brother Balarāma and his gopa friends, he spent time playing and taking cows and calves out to graze in nearby forests on the slopes of Mount Govardhan.

The gopis of Vṛndāvan were especially attracted to charming and heroic Kṛṣṇa and the melodious tunes he played on his flute. Their admiration gradually turned into love. Every morning, they would tearfully watch him taking out the cattle. Thereafter, they would be constantly thinking of him. Sometimes, they would even forget their daily chores lost in their dreamworld. They would imagine him playing his flute melodiously in the forest. They would visualise their cows and the birds, animals and other creatures of the forest listening to the wonderful notes coming from Kṛṣṇa's flute. In this way, the life of gopis became one of continuous devotion to Kṛṣṇa. The devaas and even the rishis became envious of the gopis, for there was nothing which could distract their minds away from Kṛṣṇa. Day in and day out, they were mentally with him, in a state of ecstasy.

In the twentieth chapter of the tenth canto of the Bhāgavat Purāṇ, the changes in nature as the different seasons come and go are portrayed beautifully. In continuation, the next chapter begins with a description of Kṛṣṇa, along with his friends and cows, going to the forest.

10.21.1-6: It was winter. The boys entered the woods with sylvan ponds full of clear water and a soft breeze carrying far and near the fragrance of the lotus blooms in them. As they moved gracefully forward, they heard the buzzing and strumming sounds made by bees and beetles as they hovered over the flowers, along with the happy chirpings of the birds in the forest. While grazing the cows, Kṛṣṇa took out his flute and began playing on it. As these melodious notes reached the ears of the gopis, they forgot everything in ecstasy. Their minds were filled with the image of Kṛṣṇa, draped in golden yellow silk, with peacock feathers in his hair, wearing flowers in his ears and a long floral garland hanging down from his neck, playing on his flute delightfully, adored by the gopa boys for his charm. The gopis, hearing these notes which stole their hearts, found immense joy in praising their beloved Kṛṣṇa.

The song that the gopis sing at this juncture is known as the Veṇugīta. Gathered together in groups, they glorify the transcendental song of Kṛṣṇa's flute, which enchants the whole of Vṛndāvan. They wonder, 'How fortunate are the birds and animals in the forest! They can always listen to the ravishing strains of Kṛṣṇa's flute! How lucky are the grasses and the fallen leaves and twigs on the forest floor! On them does Kṛṣṇa walk! How fortunate is his flute! It is being kissed by him whenever he is playing it!'

Veṇugīta is thus a soulful song, incorporating thirteen verses, starting from the seventh to the nineteenth śloka of this chapter. Each śloka is a short song sung by one gopi, expressing her own thought at that time.

10.21.7: 'Dear friends! The most desirable sight that eyes can behold is that of the sons of Nandagopa walking in the forest, with their friends and cows, with Kṛṣṇa playing on his divine flute and presenting us with loving sidewise glances in between.'

10.21.8: 'Kṛṣṇa, dressed in yellow silk, adorned by a garland of blue lotus flowers, wearing tender mango leaves in his ears, and peacock feathers on his hair, looks as unique as ever. Balarāma too is dressed distinctively. When these two boys are singing amidst the gopa boys surrounding them, it is as if music masters are performing, standing in the centre of the listeners.'

10.21.9: 'This flute is most fortunate, for it is freely and happily enjoying the touch of Kṛṣṇa's lips, something which is a rare experience even for us, the gopis. Seeing this, I can see the lakes and trees shedding tears of joy.'

10.21.10: 'Dear friends! This Vṛndāvan adds to the fame of the earth, for it is here that the prints of Kṛṣṇa's lotus like feet are strewn all over. Seeing peacocks dancing to the mesmerizing tunes that he plays on his flute, animals and birds of the forest stand still, as if in trance.'

10.21.11: 'These deer, even if lacking in intelligence, are so lucky for they are able to listen to the enthralling tunes emanating from Kṛṣṇa's flute. They, along with their partners, are admiring the looks of the exceptionally attired Kṛṣṇa and enjoying the tunes that he plays on his flute.'

10.21.12: 'Seeing handsome Kṛṣṇa and hearing the magical music he plays on his flute, celestial maidens, traveling in their aerial chariots overhead, get attracted to him, forget themselves and remain motionless, unaware of their robes getting loose and flowers falling from their hair.'

10.21.13: 'Cows stand still, lifting their ears erect to drink the nectar that is the music flowing from Kṛṣṇa's flute. Calves, with their tender mouths fixed on their mothers' teats, stop sucking milk to listen to the notes.'

10.21.14: 'Dear friends! Birds sitting on trees with lovely

foliage look at Kṛṣṇa unblinkingly, and listen to the melodious strains coming from his flute with full attention. These birds with such concentration power deserve to be sages!'

10.21.15: 'The speed of water-flow in rivers get reduced by whirlpools, when they become lovestruck on hearing Kṛṣṇa's flute. The rivers then offer lotus flowers blooming in them with their waves acting as hands, at the feet of the Lord.'

10.21.16: 'When Kṛṣṇa and Balarāma are walking in the sun, grazing cows in the forest, clouds in the sky hear the marvelous music arising from the flute, and spread over them as an umbrella to protect them from the hot sunrays. Flowers from the trees also fall on them to reduce the impact of the heat.'

10.21.17: 'Forest dwelling women, when they see the footprints of Kṛṣṇa on leaves of grasses, collect kumkum from them and apply it on their bodies, due to their undiluted love for him.'

10.21.18: 'The Govardhan Mountain is so lucky. He gets the opportunity to be in contact with the sacred feet of Rāma and Kṛṣṇa when they walk over him, and to serve them with ripe fruits to eat, fresh water to drink, tender grasses for their cows, and caves for them to take rest in.'

10.21.19: 'Friends, how unbelievable it is that while the brothers are treading on the forest floor, on hearing the melodious strains of Kṛṣṇa's flute, animals and birds become immobile, standing still like statues, and flowers and buds shake on the trees, forming goose pimples on them.'

Here, Veṇugīta ends. In 10.21.20, Brahmarṣi Śuka concludes by stating that the gopis, by describing the charm and līlās of Kṛṣṇa and the magic of the tunes he creates on his flute, became one with him.

CHAPTER 5

GOPĪGĪTA OR GOPIKĀGĪTA

In the tenth canto of Śrīmad Bhāgavatam, starting from the twenty ninth chapter, five chapters are devoted to the Lord's Rāsakrīda, i.e. his divine play with the gopis, his devotees of the highest order. Hence these five chapters together are referred to as 'Rāsapancādhyāyi'. How Lord Kṛṣna sent many asurās to Yamaloka (the abode of Yama, the God of Death) and how he proved his Supremacy over Brahma, Agni, Indra, and Varuna at different times are already given in earlier chapters. In the Rāsapancādhyāyi, Śrī Śuka Brahmarṣi explains to King Parīkṣit how Lord Kṛṣna defeated Manmatha, the God of Love, by his divine līlās, in the holy Vṛindāvan. Reading or listening to these five chapters is enough to help one overcome the vicious cycle of births and deaths. However, it is essential to grasp the real meaning of each word of each verse to be able to do so.

The ultimate bliss experienced by those who have become enlightened on account of penance and meditation is not different from that experienced by true devotees, who have practiced neither, but have surrendered everything to God. Gopikās of Vṛindāvan are included in this latter category.

Lord Kṛṣna was the one who conquered the God of Love; it

was not the other way round. In fact, anyone who is subdued by any emotion can never be referred to as God. Therefore, in these five chapters, what is discussed is the path to liberation adopted by true devotees through total surrender to God.

Gopikās were not ordinary earthly women. They were incarnations of sages, Apsarās, and other celestials. They had taken birth on earth by the order of the Creator to serve Lord Kṛṣna. Moreover, gopikās were not a few hundreds or thousands in number. In Padma Purāna, they are said to be one hundred and ten crores. In Śrīmad Bhāgavatam also, the same number is mentioned (10.29.44). Altogether, it would be totally wrong to conclude that Kṛṣna and the gopikās were engaged in humanly sexual play.

Lord Kṛṣna realized that the gopis had developed total detachment from all worldly affairs. So he decided to enact a divine līla with the gopis. Māya Devi, the illusory power of Mahāviṣnu, was present to play her part. Kṛṣna, more handsome than Manmatha, the God of Love, reached the banks of Kālindi (presently known as Yamuna) in all his divine splendour. There, he took out his flute and began playing magical notes on it. The melody of these enchanting notes spread far in the stillness of the night and reached the homes of the gopis.

The instant they heard the blissful notes emanating from Kṛṣna's flute, the gopis left their families and everything else behind, and ran like possessed women towards the bank of Kālindi. Nobody could hold them back. A few were forcibly held back physically; so their spirits meditated on Kṛṣna! What a blissful state they might have been in! Even for learned sages, it is not easy to be unified with God so easily.

Gopikās were mentally one with Kṛṣna at all times, including the times when they were engaged in various domestic chores. That was why leaving those chores unfinished, they ran to Kṛṣna on hearing his divine flute. No force could separate the gopis from their Lord. On seeing the Lord, the gopis' ecstasy crossed all limits. Even at that moment of total surrender of their souls, Kṛṣna decided to test them.

He addressed the gopis thus: 'Look at you! You have come running leaving behind all your household duties. Why, you have forgotten all about your parents, husbands and children and have come to me at this hour of the night! Don't you think you should not have done this? If you do not follow dharma, you will not get happiness either in this world or in the other! So go back now!'

But the gopikās were not to be dissuaded by any argument. They replied: 'The ultimate aim of a person is to be unified with God. We have left our homes and relations and wealth behind. Our aim is to be one with you. In comparison with that spiritual bliss, what is happiness in this world or the higher?'

Kṛṣna was pleased with their reply. He took them to the vast sand bank of Yamuna. They spread their shawls on the ground and sat on them. Sight of the Lord, his nearness, his touch, the fragrance of the exotic flowers in the garland he wore – in short, everything about him raised the gopis' spirits to unimaginable heights.

A shade of pride now crossed the hearts of the gopikās. Each one thought: 'Kṛṣna loves me the most! I am his darling! See how he is looking at me with his lovely eyes! How eager he is to talk to me! None can beat me in beauty or grace.'

Sensing the pride welling up in their hearts, Kṛṣna, who never lost an opportunity to rid his devotees of pride, suddenly disappeared from their midst, along with his most ardent devotee Rādha (Rādhika) who remained humble even after getting all his attention. (In the Bhāgavat Purāna, the names Radha or Rādhika do not appear. She is referred to as 'ārādhika', meaning 'worshipper'. The verse 10.30.28 starts with 'anayārādhito…' meaning 'was worshipped by her').

The other gopikās were uncontrollable in their grief. They ran here and there in search of their Lord. They roamed around the forests near Kālindi River searching for their Lord, singing loudly and calling out his name. They searched for him in the forests and caves and all possible places. Not seeing him anywhere, they wept loudly. Forgetting the fact that neither animals nor birds, nor trees nor the earth, neither the sky, nor the clouds could talk, they asked all of them the whereabouts of their beloved. Not getting any answer, they wept louder still.

Then, as if to get some solace, they began identifying themselves with Kṛṣna! Among themselves, they enacted many scenes from the life of Kṛṣna, with one gopi pretending to be Kṛṣna, and another pretending to be an asura, or Mount Govardhan or Serpent Kāliya etc.! But this also did not make them happy. Stopping all the acting, they searched for him all over again and wept afresh.

After wandering far and wide, finally they saw the footprints of their Lord, but there were footprints of a woman along with those. The gopis became doubly sad as they realized that one among them was with Kṛṣna. Soon, however, only Kṛṣna's footprints could be seen.

Actually, this was so because Rādhika, who was enjoying Kṛṣna's company, thought that she was superior to the other gopis, that Kṛṣna had chosen her as his beloved, and had spurned the others. When she became conceited thus, Kṛṣna disappeared suddenly leaving her all alone.

The tearful Rādhika wandered here and there and finally joined the other gopis. Real devotees of the Lord do not know any peace of mind until they see Him. This was the state in which the gopis found themselves now. In the end, they returned to the sand banks where Kṛṣna had left them. Addressing him directly, they sang tearfully, asking him what their fault was and why he had been so cruel to them.

This is the famous Gopīgītam or Gopikāgītam (song of the gopis) comprising nineteen heartrending ślokās (verses). This is a master piece in devotional music. According to Sage Nārada, the most ideal type of devotion is what the gopikās had for Kṛṣna. The ślokās of the Gopikāgītam should not be taken for their apparent meaning. Each verse has a hidden inner meaning which is purely spiritual. Each one is sung by one particular gopi (10.31.1-19). The meanings of these ślokās in brief are as follows:

10.31.1: "Hé Beloved! This Gokul has become the noblest of

all places as you were born here. Goddess Lakṣmi stays here at all times as she cherishes your nearness. That is why people of Bṛj remain prosperous and happy. Yet we, your servants, for whom you are our Prāṇa itself, are roaming around everywhere searching for you".

Suggested meaning – "We cannot tolerate your separation from us. Kindly see how intense our grief is. It is not right that you, who bless your devotees with joy and prosperity, are ignoring us in this way. We do not crave for any wealth. We live only for you."

The hidden meaning of this verse is that detachment from worldly objects takes one nearer to God.

10.31.2: "Hé Granter of wishes, Hé Giver of happiness! You stole charm from lotus flowers in the lake in this wintry season, and stole our hearts by looking at us with it. Isn't this equivalent to killing us, your servants, who wish for nothing materialistic from you and have surrendered to you in totality?"

Suggested meaning – "It is not true that one needs weapons to kill others. You have killed us by merely looking at us. We have no wish other than seeing you. Please come to us and remove our unbearable grief."

The underlying message of this verse is that if anyone worships God for any personal gain, he or she is not a true devotee, for there is no real love of God in such a relationship. Only devotees of the highest order have genuine love for God.

10.31.3: "Hé noble one! You saved us from poisonous waters, from Aghāsura who took the form of a python, from incessant rain and thunderstorms, from ferocious demons like Vṛsha's son Vatsa, and Maya's son Vyoma. We have been saved by you from all types of dangers many times."

Suggested meaning – "As such, is it right that now you are bent on killing us with arrows of love? If you really wanted to kill us, why did you save us from various dangers so many times?"

There is an intuition in this verse – the killing of demons Vatsa and Vyoma have not been described yet in Bhāgavatam.

Therefore, it looks as if the gopis, whose hearts are with Lord Kṛṣna at all times, could foresee what would happen in future, just like great sages.

10.31.4: "You are not just Yaśoda's son. You are a witness to what is going on in the minds of each and every living being. Oh dear friend! You have taken birth in the Yadu clan on the request of Brahma the Creator, for the benefit of mankind."

Suggested meaning – "Dear friend! We have come to know of your real nature. You are a witness to everything. So you must surely know about our present agony too. Therefore, it is not proper that you are making us sad. Please come to us, wherever you are."

This shows that the gopis knew the truth about the incarnation of Lord Viṣnu as Kṛṣna on earth. Another point to be noted is that in this verse, the gopi is addressing Kṛṣna as 'sakhe' i.e. friend. Friendship is also one type of devotion, just as servitude is, as stated in the first and second verses.

10.31.5: "Hé noblest among Vṛṣnis! Hé handsome! Please place your lotus hands, used to grant refuge to those approaching you to escape from the sorrows of this worldly existence, and used to hold the hands of Goddess Lakṣmi, on our heads in blessing."

Suggested meaning – "You remove the grief of whoever takes refuge in you; therefore it will not be difficult for you to rid us of our agony. For this, you just need appear before us – there is nothing else to be done."

The gopis want Kṛṣna to place his lotus hands on their heads as this will free them from the pangs of separation from him. To put it simply, they are craving for his nearness and his blessings.

10.31.6: "Hé astute one! Hé destroyer of the woes of the people of Bṛj! You have the power to rid us of our ego with just one smile. O friend! Do accept us. Do show us, your young devotees, the charming countenance of yours."

Suggested meaning – "Are you, who destroy the miseries of every single citizen of Bṛj, doing justice to us, when you are being cruel to us? Even if we became conceited, should you vanish like this?"

A single smile of the Lord can free the whole world of its miseries; the gopis are therefore beseeching Kṛṣna to be kind to them and appear before them with a smiling face.

10.31.7: "Taking refuge at your sacred feet, people are freed of all their sins. These are the same feet that walk along forest paths grazing cows, and are the residing place of Goddess Lakṣmi. They are the feet that danced on Kāliya's hoods, shattering his pride forever. Kindly place those lotus feet of yours on our breasts; this act will cool our hearts burning in love for you".

Suggested meaning – "You destroy the sins of anyone who worships your feet; you walk along forest paths to graze cows because of your love and affection for them; Goddess Lakṣmi, the personification of beauty, resides in your feet because of her devotion to you; and your feet danced on Kāliya's hoods as you are heroic. Please place your feet of such divinity on our breasts and extinguish our burning love."

The hidden meaning of this verse is that if God touches a person's heart, which is the residing place of lust, he or she will be freed of lust.

10.31.8: "Hé lotus-eyed one! Your speech is full of delightful sentences. The wise are enthralled by the wisdom contained in your discourse, while we are mesmerized by the love ingrained in your language. Oh heroic one! Kindly breathe life into us by sweet words emanating from your lips"

Suggested meaning – "We are nearing death because of separation from you. Only your nearness and sweet words will revive us."

By addressing the Lord as the 'heroic one', the gopis are complaining that despite possessing the divine medicine capable of bringing them back to life, why was he not administering it to them.

10.31.9: "The story of your life is amṛt in itself. This is because your glory rejuvenates the miserable, destroys all sin, and is sung by the wise. The story of your life gives unlimited joy to those who listen to it. Those who realize this truth are blessed indeed. They are the ones who perform noble acts of charity in this life."

Suggested meaning – "The nectar that is your life is nobler than the world famous nectar possessed by devas. It is because we have tasted this amṛt that we are still alive, even after being separated from you for so long. Kindly give us your darśan."

This verse makes it clear that those who have partaken kathāmṛt (the nectar that is the Lord's stories) which destroys the roots of karmas, are liberated from the vicious cycle of birth and death and attain mokṣa.

10.31.10: "However, O Beloved, only listening to your glory will not give us peace, because our minds have become turbulent thinking of your līlās. Your smile, loving looks, and endearing speech are churning our minds."

Suggested meaning – "We cannot remain peaceful if you are not near us. Why are you keeping away from us, despite knowing our present condition?"

The underlying meaning of this verse is that the devoted can meditate on any of the aspects of the Lord mentioned.

10.31.11: "Hé master! We always worry that your feet, soft and beautiful like lotus flowers, will be hurt by stones and sharp tips of grass while walking along forest paths."

Suggested meaning - "Our minds get agitated in this way whenever you leave for the forests."

How much the gopis care for Kṛṣna and how they are pained whenever they think he is hurt, is unbelievable.

10.31.12: "Yet, when we see you return in the evenings, with dust particles from the hooves of cattle sticking on your charming lotus-like face partly covered by your deep blue curly locks, you immerse us again in the warmth of love."

Suggested meaning – "You know that you arouse such feelings in us. Why are you still not appearing in front of us?"

The gopis are so much in love with their Lord that they recall each and every detail of his appearance and feel saddened all the more at his absence from their midst.

10.31.13: "Oh beloved! Your lotus soft feet, which remove all sorrows of those who surrender unto you, are worshipped even by the Creator. Your feet are an ornament to the earth, are meditated upon during times of distress, and provide supreme happiness and peace of mind to all. Please place such divine feet of yours on our breasts."

Suggested meaning – "If you do as we say, our minds will become calm and we will attain great happiness".

The verse proves beyond doubt that the gopis have surrendered themselves unto Kṛṣna. Their ultimate wish is that Kṛṣna should remain in their hearts; this alone will make them happy.

10.31.14: "Not only that, Oh Heroic one, please give us your lips equivalent to amṛt, which destroy grief and enhance joy, which are kissing your flute whenever you play on it, and which make people forget all other desires of theirs."

Suggested meaning – "Your lips are divine beyond description; please kiss us with those lips".

Even Lord Kṛṣna's flute is fortunate enough to be in contact with his lips. So there is nothing wrong in the gopis wishing for the same.

10.31.15: "Whenever you are wandering in the forests of Vṛndāvan, we are not able to see you. Those moments appear like long ages to us. At all times, we long to see your charming face, made more beautiful by long locks of curly hair. As such, we assume that whoever has made eyelids for eyes must be quite stupid!"

Suggested meaning – "Seeing you gives us ultimate joy while not seeing you pushes us down into depths of sorrow. This is why we have come to you, giving up the whole world."

Just like those who have given up everything for God realization, the gopis have gone to Lord Kṛṣna as they cannot remain without seeing him even for a second.

10.31.16: "Hé Acyuta! Disregarding the words of our husbands, children other relatives and elders, we have come to you, attracted by your flute. How can you cheat us by leaving us at night like this?"

Suggested meaning – "Attracting us first by playing on your flute and then discarding us in this manner is nothing short of cheating us. You knew very well that we love only you. So how can you do this to us?"

The gopis are telling the Lord that no relationships in the world are permanent and only he can give ultimate joy to them. It is in this knowledge that they have gone to him, leaving all others behind. In such a situation, if he disowns them, what will happen to them?

10.31.17: "We have seen again and again in solitude your smiling face and your broad chest, the residing place of Goddess Lakṣmi. We have seen how you look at us with love and affection. This increases our love for you all the more."

Suggested meaning – "We cannot bear the thought that such intense love of ours is being spurned by you."

They are complaining that in solitude, Kṛṣna fascinated them by his looks and actions and convinced them of his love for them; and now they only have one desire – and that is to see him again.

10.31.18: "The objective of your incarnation is to remove the grief of the people of Bṛj and the forests nearby. It is in fact for ushering in good days for the entire mankind. We long only for your nearness; by your remaining away from us, we are becoming mentally ill. Give us suitable medicines for this condition."

Suggested meaning – "You know very well what medicine we need for our present condition, and that is your presence. Please give this medicine to us, which we are yearning for, without delay."

Lord Kṛṣna knows what medicine is required to make the gopis well. It is giving himself to them, for they wish for nothing else. Their only desire is to be one with Kṛṣna, the Supreme Being.

10.31.19: "Though we are afraid that you may hurt your soft and delicate feet if you place them on our hard breasts, please do so. You may place them softly, and we shall be delighted. At the same time, we cannot bear the thought that you are at this moment walking along the forest paths full of thorns, which are sure to injure your soft feet. You are our life itself; we cannot bear the thought of your feet getting hurt."

Suggested meaning – "We are alive because you live in our hearts. Our love to you is total. We cannot even imagine you getting hurt. Please come back to us."

The gopis are immersed in sorrow thinking of the hardships Kṛṣna is going through in the forest. This shows the intensity of their love to him. It is just indescribable.

When the gopis were lamenting thus, singing Gopika Gītam loudly, Kṛṣna suddenly appeared among them, radiant as ever. The gopis were so happy and excited that they did not know what to do. Some just looked at him as if to imprint his figure permanently in their minds, some held his hands while some nestled closer to him. His mere presence had electrified the whole atmosphere.

Thereafter, Kṛṣna played with them in the forests, and in the clear waters of Kālindi, taking them to great heights of bliss. Then, the Master of the Universe invited the gopis to dance. He then transformed himself into many Kṛṣnās! This multiplicity was his divine illusion. Nevertheless, every gopi was happy that she had her own Kṛṣna. There were as many Kṛṣnās as there were gopis. All stood in a circle, each gopi paired with her Lord, and began dancing.

The celestials lined up in the sky to watch this rare event. They sounded bugles, beat drums and sang melodious songs. The pairs moved round and round in measured steps. Drops of perspiration shone like pearls on the gopis' faces. Their knots of hair loosened, and flowers adorning their hair dropped down on the ground. Their garments swayed and earrings jingled rhythmically. They sang and clapped and merrily hugged each other. As the speed of their dance increased steadily, the gopis were mentally transported to an entirely different ethereal world of spiritual ecstasy.

This is the famous Rāsa Dance. The Devās, apsarās, gandharvās and other celestials watched this unique dance from above in rapturous joy and showered flowers on the dancers. They remained entranced, experiencing the joy of being in that blissful state of oneness with the Lord. The dance went on till dawn. As it ended, the entire world was filled with an indescribable bliss. Gradually, stars became dimmer and dimmer. The eastern sky turned red with the rise of Aruna, indicating the approaching sunrise. Lotus buds began to bloom revealing their beautiful petals. Birds chirping happily left their nests and flew away in different directions. Only then did Kṛṣna take leave of the gopis; after which they all went back home.

The episodes of Rāsakrīda and Rāsa Dance in which we see Kṛṣna playing and dancing with the gopis should be understood in the right sense. First of all, it should be kept in mind that Kṛṣna was just a boy who was eleven years of age at that time. More important than this is the central theme of the whole act. The gopikās are the jīvātmās always in search of the Paramātma. When they succeed in their search, they experience limitless joy. The unification of the jīvātma (individual soul) with the Paramātma (the soul of the universe, i.e., the Supreme Being) is the ultimate aim of every human being. That was exactly what the gopis achieved by their spotless devotion. This is the explanation provided by many scholars.

Mahāviṣnu is the Master of Māya (illusion), which binds the mortals. All living beings are affected by their respective karmās, but Viṣnu is not bound by the effect of karma. For Him, fulfilling the wishes of His devotees is all that matters. In the Rāsakrīda and Rāsa Dance, He did exactly that. It was by His own Māya that He appeared as enjoying with the gopis.

Here, we can see how God listens to the call of His devotees. There may be trials and tribulations in between, but ultimately, devotees are rewarded by God. We see examples of this in our everyday life too, even in this Kaliyug.

CHAPTER 6

YUGALAGĪTA

Balarāma, Kṛṣna and their companions gradually entered the third pancaka (age 11-15 years) of their lives. Kṛṣna obviously was the darling of the entire Vṛndāvan. The gopis were especially attracted to him. They were seeing him and listening to his heroic deeds day in and day out. Every morning, they would tearfully watch him taking out the cattle. Thereafter they would be constantly thinking of him. In the afternoon, the gopis would assemble in groups and talk about him and sing bhajans and kīrtans in his praise. As evenings came, they would go out of their houses to their courtyards and wait for Kṛṣna's return. In this way, there was nothing which could distract their minds away from Kṛṣna. Day and night, they were mentally one with him, in a state of ecstasy.

Still, at the same time, the gopis were suffering intense agony too. This grief of the gopis after Kṛṣna's leaving for the forest to tend cows is described in what is known as 'Yugalagītam' in the thirty fifth chapter of the tenth canto of the Bhāgavat Purāna. In the first śloka of the chapter, Maharṣi Śuka explains the situation thus:

10.35.1: While Kṛṣna went to the forest, the hearts and minds of the gopis followed him there. They sang about the various līlās of Kṛṣna and spent their days in gloom.

Thereafter, the Yugalagītam begins. It comprises twenty four ślokās (10.35.2-10.35.25). Two ślokās together form one sentence. This is why it is called 'Yugalagītam' (Yugalam in Sanskrit means a pair). Each set is sung by one gopi. The last śloka of the chapter (10.35.26) gives the conclusion given by the Maharṣi.

In the beginning of Yugalagītam, one gopi describes in one śloka the words and actions of the celestial maidens on seeing Lord Kṛṣna and continues the narrative in the next śloka, thereby completing the couplet.

10.35.2: "Hé Gopis! When we see Kṛṣna standing gracefully resting his left cheek on his left palm, with eyebrows trembling softly and beautifully, and hear him playing flute kept on his lips by opening and closing the holes in it with his delicate fingers,

10.35.3: "then we, the maidens of the devaloka, along with the sidhās, are mesmerized. Our minds get stirred by the God of Love and we become shy."

Listening to this, another gopi says that there is nothing strange in the celestial maidens getting attracted by Lord Kṛṣna. She then proceeds to give an account of her own observation, in the next two verses.

10.35.4: "Hé friends! Listen to this amazing phenomenon – when Śrī Kṛṣna, in whose garland there always exists a sweet smile, who has a permanent lightning in his chest, and who entertains us grieving women, starts playing melodious notes on his flute,

10.35.5: "then, herds of cows and bulls of Bṛj, attracted by the divine notes of the flute from far away, stop chewing cud and stand still with sharpened ears and closed eyes, as if asleep, looking like a painting."

A third gopi says that not just living beings, even non-living entities are affected by the notes played by Kṛṣna on his flute.

10.35.6: "Sometimes, when Sri Kṛṣna, adorned in peacock

feathers and accompanied by gopa boys walks with Balarāma, both brothers wearing green leaves like wrestlers, calls the cows,

10.35.7: "then, like us who are unfortunate and who keep waiting for the dust from his lotus feet get blown to us by wind, rivers sway their arms on account of their love to him and remain still."

Another gopi now describes how the trees are affected by Kṛṣna's flute.

10.35.8: "When Kṛṣṇa, always accompanied by the gopa boys eulogizing his heroic deeds, like Goddess Lakṣmi who is always with Lord Viṣnu, calls on his flute, the cows wandering along the hilly terrains by their names,

10.35.9: then, wonder of wonders! The trees and climbers in the forest, full of love for him, become so immersed in joy that their branches bend down due to the weight of their innumerable flowers and fruits, and shower below drops of nectar."

Yet another gopi then describes how the melodious notes on Lord Kṛṣna's flute attracted various birds in the forest.

10.35.10: "When he, wearing a beautiful bindi, became one with his flute by putting his lips to it, and played heavenly notes on it, as if respecting the beetles who were buzzing loudly, intoxicated by the nectar from the flowers of the heavenly fragrant basil in his floral garland,

10.35.11: then, amazing! Attracted by the melodious tunes being played on Sri Kṛṣna's flute, the swans and plovers in the lakes, having found quietude of mind, closed their eyes and prayed to him silently."

Another gopika has this to say:

10.35.12: "Hé beautiful women of Bṛj! When Sri Kṛṣna, wearing flowers and glowing with charm, stands happily near the mountain ranges along with Balarāma, and begins to fill the earth with the joyful notes of his flute,

10.35.13: "then, clouds in the sky produce soft thunder as accompaniment to Kṛṣna's flute; they do not want the thunder to be loud as it would drown the songs being played on the flute;

they also shower fine misty drops like flowers on Kṛṣna and spread a cool shade on him, like an umbrella."

Continues another gopi:

10.35.14: "Hé chaste Yaśode! When your son, an expert in playing games with other gopa boys, and who is a self-taught master in flute, keeps his flute on his beautiful red lips and controls the emanating notes expertly,

10.35.15: "then, hearing this heavenly music, noble gods like Indra, Śiva, Brahma and others, despite being distinct in their specific competences, lower their heads and are lost in its divinity, forgetting everything else."

Yet another gopi says:

10.35.16: "When he who brings solace to the ground of Bṛj hurt by the hard hooves of the cows and calves by treading on it majestically like an elephant, with soles marked by the unique symbols of a flag, thunderbolt, lotus flower and an ankuśam (hook for guiding elephants), took out his flute and played on it,

10.35.17: "then, we, in a state of bliss looking at the loving eyes of Kṛṣna, were brought under the spell of Manmatha, the God of Love, and were transfixed to the ground like trees, conscious of neither dress nor hair as we were in a trance."

Yet another gopi now described how doe and deer reacted to Kṛṣna's flute.

10.35.18: "When once Kṛṣna, who was wearing a garland made of fragrant basil leaves, and who had tied bells around the necks of cows to count them with ease, placed his arm on his friend's shoulder and began playing on his flute,

10.35.19: "then, the doe of the forest, enchanted by the flute's notes, left their respective husband deer, and ignoring their homes and food, like the gopis, remained near Kṛṣna."

Another gopi gives an account of what Kṛṣna does after grazing the cows in the evening.

10.35.20: "Oh sinless one! When your son, the son of Nanda, decorated in festive jasmine garlands and surrounded by gopa boys and cows sported in the waters of Yamuna, giving great joy to his friends,

10.35.21: "then, a soft breeze, like the fragrance of sandalwood, fanned him; celestials who sing praise of gods stood all around him and served him by singing songs, playing musical instruments and showering flowers on him."

Yet another gopi describes the homeward journey of Kṛṣna.

10.35.22: "For what purpose Kṛṣna had lifted the mountain (Govardhan), that is the same purpose for which he does everything good to us, the cows of Bṛj, and he is the one whose feet are worshipped by the age old Brahma. On his way back home at the end of each day, he collects the cows while playing his flute; he is the one admired by all his friends and followers.

10.35.23: "Here comes Kṛṣna, who is glowing due to the work done the whole day, whose garlands are covered in dust raised by the hooves of the cows, whose sight gives great joy to the beholders and who is ever desirous of performing charitable acts, who has got the good wishes of all his friends, and who was conceived in Devaki's womb." (The indication is towards Yaśoda here as she is the wife of Nanda, also known as Devaka).

All the gopis are ecstatic on seeing Kṛṣna approaching them.

10.35.24: "See, his eyeballs are moving due to his love for us. He is wearing a floral garland, his face is charming like the full moon, and the glow of his soft cheeks is enhanced by the brightness of his gold studs.

10.35.25: "Here comes Sri Kṛṣna, like the moon rising happily at twilight. He is approaching us, freeing us the gopis of Bṛj of our intense sorrow throughout the day due to separation from him."

Here ends the Yugalagītam. Śrī Śuka concludes this set of verses in the last verse of the chapter thus:

10.35.26: "In this way, oh King Parīkṣit, the gopikās of Bṛj, fully immersed in their love of Sri Kṛṣna, always engrossed in his thoughts, sang songs about him in joy during the daytime too."

With this verse, the thirty fifth chapter of the tenth canto of the divine Bhāgavat Purān comes to an end.

CHAPTER 7

VIRAHAGĪTA

Kṛṣṇa had killed many Asurās by now, all emissaries of Kamsa. One day, Sage Nārada went to Mathura and met Kamsa. The sage described to Kamsa in detail the miraculous deeds done by Kṛṣṇa. He then concluded: "Kṛṣṇa, incarnation of Viṣṇu on earth, is the son of Vasudeva and Devaki. Yaśoda is not his real mother. Neither is Nanda his real father. Kṛṣṇa, whom you have been searching everywhere, is the eighth son of Devaki. Only if you kill Kṛṣṇa and his brother Rāma, can you live peacefully." With this advice, Nārada went away.

Kamsa was aghast. Immediately, he sent two more Asurās to kill the brothers. Then, as a back up, he made another plan. He decided to organise a yagya in Mathura for which the boys would be invited. At the entrance of the palace, he would get them trampled under the heavy feet of the biggest elephant of Mathura! In case they escaped this trap and did enter the palace, two of his best wrestlers, Cāṇūra and Muṣṭika, would challenge them for wrestling, and put Rāma and Kṛṣṇa to death!

After making all these arrangements, without any delay, Kamsa sent for Akrūra, who was a friend of the Yādavās. To him, Kamsa said, "I am organising a dhanuryagya to invoke Lord Śiva in the royal bow. Go to Gokul, and on my behalf, invite Nandagopa, Kṛṣṇa and Balarāma for the yagya. Start tomorrow itself."

Akrūra immediately guessed that Kamsa was inviting them with bad intentions. However, he had to obey his master. He therefore started on his journey immediately. A great devotee of Kṛṣṇa, he was sure that wicked Kamsa's end was near. Happy at this thought, and also happy at the opportunity of seeing the Lord, Akrūra sped in his chariot to Gokul, and reached there by dusk.

Kṛṣṇa and Rāma saw him first, and they led him into their house. There he told Nandagopa the purpose of his visit. It was soon decided that father and sons would proceed to Mathura the next day itself.

The gopis soon came to know of this, and were distraught. They could not fathom how they were going to endure this separation from Kṛṣṇa. They were uncontrollable in their grief. They formed small groups, wept pitiably and poured out their feelings freely. These outpourings together is known as Virahagīta. It comprises thirteen ślokās, starting from the nineteenth śloka to the thirty first, of the thirty ninth chapter of the tenth canto.

10.39.19: "Alas! How cruel you are, Oh Creator! You let people meet each other and make them love each other. Then, before they are fully satisfied, you separate them. Why you are doing so is beyond anybody's comprehension. This is like games that immature children play.

10.39.20: "It is unkind enough when you do this to common people. It is more so when it is in the case of Kṛṣṇa. For, after showing us the most attractive face of Kṛṣṇa, with a bewitching smile that destroy's one's sorrows, you snatch that vision away from us.

10.39.21: "It must be you, Oh Creator, who has come here as Akrūra, to take Kṛṣṇa away from us. Kṛṣṇa embodies the beauty of the whole universe; and we are aware of this truth. Are you envious of us for realizing this truth?

10.39.22: "We have given up our homes and families, including our parents, husbands and children, and have taken refuge in him. We are immensely grieved at his leaving us like this now. Alas, he is not even looking at us, despite knowing our state of mind.

10.39.23: "Tomorrow morning, the women of Mathura will have the fortune of beholding the charming face of Kṛṣṇa. They will joyfully feast their eyes on the charismatic smile on his face.

10.39.24: "Kṛṣṇa will also be fascinated by the damsels of Mathura as they are sure to attract his attention by their bewitching smiles and sweet words. How then will he remember us, the rustic maidens of Vṛndāvan?

10.39.25: "It will be a visual feast for the devotees of Kṛṣṇa in Mathura. They will savour the vision of Devaki's son Kṛṣṇa, the one who makes even Mahālakṣmi happy beyond words, and in whom all good qualities reside.

10.39.26: "It is this Akrūra who is the cause of all our grief. Who named this krūr (cruel) man Akrūra? He is taking Kṛṣṇa away from us without even bothering to try to console us. He is a most horrible man.

10.39.27: "He is getting into the chariot, and the young gopas who will be also going to Mathura in other vehicles along with, are hurrying him up. The elderly gopas are keeping quiet. On the whole, we are the ones affected in the worst possible manner.

10.39.28: "We are unable to be remain separate from him for even half a second. So, even the elderly of the village cannot prevent us from protesting against our loved one leaving us.

10.39.29: "Hé gopis! The time we spent in his company had passed so very rapidly. It feels like just a few seconds. When this is the case, how can we let him go away from us? How will we endure his absence amidst us?

10.39.30: "From the jungles of Vṛndāvan, he comes back to Bṛj every evening, surrounded by Balarāma and his gopa friends, with dust from the hooves of the cows sticking to his curly hair, playing his flute. His sidewise glances to us, wrapped in a loving smile, steal our hearts. How can we live without him?"

Here, the Virahagīta ends.

In 10.39.31, Śrī Śuka Brahmarṣi says that in this way, alas, the gopis, whose hearts were fixed in Kṛṣṇa, wept loudly, and without feeling ashamed, called out his names aloud, "Govinda! Dāmodara! Mādhava!"

While the gopis were lamenting thus, Akrūra's chariot moved forward, as Kṛṣṇa mounted in it. The vehicles of others followed, all of them together making a caravan. The gopis watched everything and crying loudly, ran after the chariot.

Kṛṣṇa turned back, and smiled at them. Seeing the gopis' intense anguish, he consoled them by sending an emissary to them then and there, with the message, "I shall return soon. Do not grieve."

The caravan moved on. The gopis stood transfixed till the tip of the flag on Akrūra's chariot vanished from sight and dust raised by the caravan settled far away. With their minds completely absorbed in Kṛṣna, they stood as still as figures in a painting until they could no longer see the chariot. Then, singing Kṛṣna's glories, they sorrowfully returned to their respective homes and spent days and nights, their thoughts fixed on Kṛṣṇa.

CHAPTER 8

BHRAMARAGĪTA

At the age of twelve, Kṛṣna killed Kamsa, made his father Ugrasena King of Mathura, and stayed on there for some time.

One day, Kṛṣna called his friend and devotee Uddhava and told him, "Go to Gokul, dear friend, and meet my parents Nandagopa and Yaśoda, give them all my news and make them happy. Also, meet the gopis and remove their grief in being separated from me by consoling them. The gopis' minds are forever fixed in me for they have given up everything else in the world. At this time, as I am far away, they have become indifferent to even their daily chores. Meet them, pacify them, give then my message, and enlighten them spiritually on my behalf."

Uddhava was the disciple of Bṛhaspati, the devaguru. He was very wise, and was the chief minister of the Yādavās. He reached Gokul at sunset. He went straight to Nandagopa's house and spent the night there. Nanda was very happy to see him not only as he was an old friend, but also because he had brought the latest news about Kṛṣṇa. He recollected for long the exploits of his son, and shed tears, thinking of him. Yaśoda participated in the discussions and became misty eyed too. The three rejoiced at the mere thought of Kṛṣṇa. 'Uddhavam' also means festival.

The presence of Uddhava truly ushered in a festive mood in Nandagopa's house.

It was the next morning that the gopis saw Uddhava. They had seen an unknown chariot the previous evening, but had not known who had come in it. They were hoping that it might be someone from Mathura with Kṛṣna's news. When the gopis saw the lotus-eyed Uddhava, dressed in yellow silk, wearing sparkling ornaments and a garland of flowers like their Kṛṣṇa, they were overjoyed. They ran to him, and paid respects to him. Surrounding Uddhava on all sides, they began conversing with him.

"Sir," started one gopi, "was it not Kṛṣṇa who sent you to Gokul? He must have told you to meet his father and mother. That must be the only connection he has with Gokul."

Another continued, "Other than that with parents, all relationships are in fact superficial. They remain only as long as the need is there. It is just like the association between flowers and beetles. Bees and beetles fly away from flowers as soon as there is no nectar left in them."

"Students leave the teacher when their studies are over. Birds fly away from trees when the fruits are over. Animals leave forests which get burnt in a fire. In short, when the purpose of the bond is over, one forgets his friends and relations. Has Kṛṣṇa forgotten us, his childhood friends?" wept another gopi.

"How can we ever forget the happy times we spent here in his pleasant company? We are spending our days and nights now thinking of him and him only. When will he come back?" wailed a fourth gopi.

In this way, the gopis kept on asking him questions and weeping at the same time. They described to him the happy days in Gokul spent with Kṛṣṇa, and how they had lost all interest in life after he had gone to Mathura. They sang bhajans and kīrtans about their beloved Kṛṣṇa and cried bitterly, unable to bear separation from him.

In the midst of the gopis who were thus lamenting, a bhramaram (beetle) flew down. One of the gopis observed the similarity in complexion between the beetle and Kṛṣna. She imagined that the beetle was Kṛṣna's messenger. So she began talking to the beetle; the other gopis did likewise. In this way, they related to Uddhava all that they wanted to convey to him. These verses make the 'Bhramaragītam'. It comprises ten verses, included in the forty seventh chapter of the tenth canto – 10.47.12 to 10.47.21.

10.47.12: "Hé nectar drinker! Your complexion is similar to Kṛṣna, you must be his friend. However, do not touch our feet because your hair is full of kumkum from the flowers worn by other women with whom Sri Kṛṣna was in contact. Let him please them and remain in the Yādava court. Such a person has sent you here. What a messenger you are!

10.47.13: "The one who is like you gave us the nectar of his lips only once; after that he left us and went away. That one occasion was enough to make us forget ourselves. We do not understand how Goddess Lakṣmi serves his lotus feet; must surely be because she has also lost her heart to him, influenced by his sweet words.

10.47.14: "Hé beetle! Why are you singing songs about Kṛṣna, who is now the King of Yadus to us, the homeless? Sing about the glory of Kṛṣna to his present women friends (in Mathura). They will fulfil your wishes. What can we do for you?

10.47.15: "He who can attract any woman on the earth, in the heaven and in the nether world by his sweet smile and just a movement of his eye brows; the dust under whose feet is worshipped by the goddess of wealth, loved us also earlier as he is famous as one who helps the weak and needy.

10.47.16: "You have come from Śrī Kṛṣna; as such, you know all his tricks. I know that you have come to console me with sweet words and convince me. I have given up all worldly connections and even desire for heaven for his sake; yet he has forgotten me. As such, what is there to talk about? Leave my feet.

10.47.17: "Like you, Kṛṣna is also dark in complexion. Like a hunter, he (Sri Rāma) killed a monkey king (Bāli). Infatuated by a woman (Sīta), he maimed another woman (Sūrpaṇakha).

He (Vāmana) tied down his devotee (Mahābali), who was performing a sacrifice to go to heaven, and sent him to the nether land. In short, friendship with the dark is enough. In spite of all this, I just cannot forget him. What to do?

10.47.18: "Those sad and grieving people, who drink even one drop of the nectar that is the story and līlās of Kṛṣna, get totally detached from all worldly relations, leave their homes and families, and like birds which are free to roam around anywhere, lead the life of ascetics.

10.47.19: "Like ignorant does, female blackbucks and antelopes, who fall prey to the hunter that traps them with his music, we have been lured by Kṛṣna's sweet words into loving him. The result is that we have to endure intense pangs of separation from him, as hard as the touch of his nails. Therefore, hey messenger, tell us some news other than Kṛṣna's."

When the beetle comes back after flying away for some time, the gopi is asking him:

10.47.20: "Dear friend, have you come back again, sent to us by Kṛṣna, whom we love most intensely? Hé revered one! If that is so, we accept you in our midst. Ask us whatever you want. We shall give it to you. However, Hé innocent one, how can you take us to him, our foe, when his wife Goddess Lakṣmi is residing in his chest at all times?"

Finally, the gopis regain their composure and ask the beetle whatever they want to know about Kṛṣna.

10.47.21: "We are happy to see you. Is our Lord still in Mathura? Does he remember his parents and other relatives, their houses, and the gopa boys? Does he speak anything about us, his servant maids? Will he ever place his hand, more fragrant than musk, on our heads?"

Here ends the Bhramaragīta. Uddhava was amazed to see this total devotion of these rustic village women. In whatever they saw in or around them, nothing existed except the Lord.

"You have surrendered your hearts to the Lord. So you will be worshipped by all. Devotion to the Lord can be achieved by charity, penance, sacrifices, chanting his names, learning the Vedās, practising Aṣtānga Yoga etc. Yet you have achieved what even great sages cannot accomplish, by your absolute love and devotion to the Lord. What more is there to attain in this world? Your fortune is indescribable. Your grief because of separation from your Lord has been a blessing for me, for I got an opportunity to come here and see you and realize what real bhakti is."

Therafter, Uddhava proceeded to give the gopis Kṛṣṇa's message to them. He said, "Do not for a moment think that Kṛṣṇa has forgotten you. He has told me to specially convey to you this message that all of you are always in his thoughts. Kṛṣṇa told me that he cannot be separated from you as he is within you. Physically, you are far from him and so memories are torturing you, but you should think of him and always be devoted to him. You will soon be one with him." Uddhava then proceeded to relate Kṛṣna's special message to the gopis, revealing to them the secret of life. Thus did Uddhava console the gopis and enlighten them.

Uddhava stayed on at Gokul for many days enjoying the hospitality of the gopaas, joyfully watching the gopis' devotion towards Kṛṣṇa. In fact, he considered the whole of Gokul a holy place as the gopis, Kṛṣṇa's true devotees, were treading on the earth there. He paid respect to the footprints of the gopis because by this time he had come to know that nobody could match them in devotion to the Lord.

Later, Uddhava took leave of everyone at Gokul and returned to Mathura. It is said that one main reason why Kṛṣna sent Uddhava to Gokul was to let him see and experience for himself the total devotion of the gopis.

CHAPTER 9

ŚRUTI GĪTA

The eighty seventh chapter of the tenth canto of Śrīmad Bhāgavat Purān comprises the Śruti Gita, also known as Veda-Stuti, along with its introduction and conclusion. At the beginning of this chapter, in the 1st verse, i.e. 10.87.1., we see King Parīkṣit asking Brahmarṣi Śuka, "Hé knower of all! How do the Śrutis (Vedās) explain 'Brahman' which is beyond the good and the bad, as it lacks any Guṇās?"

Maharṣi Śuka answers this question thus:

10.87.2: "God created intellect, sense organs, mind and breath for Jīvās, which are parts of Himself, to experience sensual pleasures, perform good deeds for progress in life, attain heaven and other such lokās, in the form of their souls, as a result of their good deeds, and get freed from the vicious cycle of birth and death.

10.87.3: "This is how the upaniṣads explained Brahmaṁ or Brahman. This is what our good ancestors understood and accepted. Those who understand and accept this truth will finally achieve detachment and attain salvation."

To explain the real meaning of Brahman as per the śrutis,

Maharṣi Śuka narrated a story at this juncture.

10.87.4: "Hé King! I shall now narrate to you the story of a dialogue beween Sage Nārada and Sage Nārāyana. The listener was Nārada and the speaker was Nārāyana.

10.87.5: "Once, Sage Nārada, who loves travelling in all the worlds, went to visit Sage Nārāyana in his hermitage.

10.87.6: "Which Sage Nārāyana remains in this land of Bharata doing penance righteously and correctly for the well-being of humanity,

10.87.7: "in his hermitage in the village by name Kalāpa, seated in the centre surrounded by many sages, Sage Nārada asked him the same question that you have asked me now.

10.87.8: "In the presence of Ṛṣis all around, Sage Nārāyana answered this question, citing the instance of the discussion on this topic among sages long back.

10.87.9: Śrī Nārāyana told Nārada, "Hé son of Brahma! Long back, in the world of humans, some learned sages who were strict adherents of severe penance and who were born out of the mind of Brahma (meaning Sanaka and his brothers) were engaged in a Brahmasatram.

10.87.10: "That Brahmasatram took place at a time you had gone to visit Aniruddha, the king of Śweta Island. In that Satram, everything about Brahman—its qualitative and non-qualitative aspects—were discussed and a conclusion reached. That dialogue can clear all your doubts regarding Brahman.

10.87.11: "Those sages (Sanaka and his brothers) were all equally well-informed, with similar prowess in penance, and with good conducts. They saw Brahman in all the creation. In a Brahmasatram, scholars who converse about Brahman are all identical in knowledge. Yet in this Satram, by mutual consent, one of them was designated as the speaker and others as listeners.

10.87.12: Sanandana said, "The entire nature incorporating all that was created, was dissolved at the end of the great deluge. At that time, Īśwara was in yoga-nidra. Then, Śruti Devatās, originated from the first breath of God, woke Him up by uttering the Veda vākyās describing Him.

10.87.13: "This was like the office staff of a palace waking up an emperor in the morning, praising his glory and adventure by narrating suitable incidents."

From the next verse onwards, it is Śrutigīta. Here, the Śrutis start acclaiming His qualities. This famous Gīta of the Bhāgavat Purāna comprises twenty eight ślokās and spans from the fourteenth verse to the forty first one.

10.87.14: The Śrutis said, "Hé unconquerable Lord! Victory to you! The real blissful self of all that is present in the universe, living or non-living, is bound by Nature, and only you can release them from binding with Nature.

10.87.15: "Earthen pots are made of earth and go back to earth; likewise, even gods are born out of you, and later dissolve in you. This shows that you are the only cause for everyone and everything. Only Brahman is present forever. This is just like the fact that even though a person is standing on anything on the Earth, he is indirectly dependent on the Earth for a foothold. Realizing this truth, Ṛṣis surrender everything to you as you are the base of all.

10.87.16: "Hé Master of the three Guṇās! Those who are aware of this truth take bath in the ocean of nectar, which is the collection of your stories that washes all past sins away, and consequently, are saved from future sins and become pure. Such purified devotees pray to you, the giver of eternal bliss.

10.87.17: "If men pray to you, their living is meaningful; otherwise, their life is without purpose. If a person does not pray to God, thereby disbanding his sins and purifying his mind, and does not contemplate on the ultimate truth by thinking beyond his body's covering known as Pancakośa consisting of five layers, i.e. annamaya kośa, prānamaya kośa, manonmaya kośa, vijnānamaya kośa and ānandamaya kośa, thereby realising God, his life as a human being has no meaning. It is just like a bellow which blows air in and out; this is however not breathing.

10.87.18: "Different Ṛṣis follow different systems. Among them, those who are not fully enlightened concentrate only on Maṇipura Chakra inner to the navel during meditation. However, those who can see through the ultimate truth, like the Ṛṣis following the ārani system concentrate their minds on you, the bright light glowing within their hearts, and in the end, their souls move through the suṣumna or the spinal cord and leave their bodies through the brahmarandhra, a fine pore at the center of the top of the head, so that they need not return to this mortal world again.

10.87.19: "Ignorant Jīvās suffer endless sorrows because they consider the mortal lives to be real. Truth is that each Jīva is entering into a series of mortal lives—high or low, good or bad—as a result of his own deeds in the past life. When a Jīva accumulates enough puṇya by his lack of desire in this and other worlds, when his dispassion increases and when he realizes that the universe is a myth, he escapes from his ignorant state of existence and becomes one with God.

10.87.20: "There are many types of bodies as decided by their respective previous karmas; but human body is the noblest of all. Man has the capacity to know and perform all deeds as explained in the Vedās. Man can contemplate on the truth and realize what exactly his real self is and attain salvation with that knowledge. Oh God, those who are wise and have understood this truth take refuge in you and achieve ultimate success in life.

10.87.21: "Hé Īśwara! Such Jīvās are immersed in the ocean of nectar that is Your, the Supreme Being's, līla. You bless the universe by being born as various creatures to make them understand the ultimate spiritual truth. Such Jīvās do not wish for any material pleasure. They give up everything and covet for not even mokṣa. They spend their lives, along with other devotees, worshipping the feet of God.

10.87.22: "In spite of getting human birth, in which a person can act as per God's will and consider God as friend and relative, some Jīvās do not love God or follow His will – this is most unfortunate. Alas, such unwise people, who do not worship God in spite of getting human bodies, forgetting Him who is affectionate and always ready to help, and be in the company of bad people, are born as lowly creatures after their death. This is equivalent to suicide.

10.87.23: "Learned yogis attain you by controlling their minds, prāṇa, intellect, and senses. Women attain you by attaching themselves to you in love, while enemies attain you by constant hatred. There are thus different pathways to reach God. We the Śrutis also worship you, who are present everywhere.

10.87.24: "You have neither a beginning nor an end. How will the mortal man know your greatness? From you the Supreme Being, Brahma came into existence first, and from Him, the Devās. It was after this that other creatures came into being. During creation, no one can know about God as they are being created. During dissolution, the whole universe disbands in Him; at that time also, none can know the real nature of God. In between creation and dissolution, only those who overcome the various obstacles in the path to liberation realize God. Neither Time nor the Śāstrās can help men in this matter. In short, God Himself has to will that a person realizes Him.

10.87.25: "Believing that the illusory world originated because of a cause, or that the nature of the soul is dual, or that results of karma are permanent – all such views are against what we, the Śrutis, declare. All these theories result from bhram or ignorance. Even some precepts are victims of such misunderstandings. In the eyes of a truly knowledgeable person, nothing exists other than Brahman.

10.87.26: "Universe is an imagination of the mind which has three Guṇās. Thus, in fact, universe as such does not exist. The wise know that only Brahman has existence. Such a person sees only Brahman in the universe, just like he sees only gold in the various types of ornaments made of gold.

10.87.27: "Those who depend wholly on you and pray to you conquer death by your blessings – by the grace of you who know everything. After death, they become one with you. Others are attacked by death like an animal, even if they are illustrious in all other aspects. Those who love you get purified, and not others.

10.87.28: "You are above aspects like mind, intellect etc. Yet you are omnipotent and complete in yourself. Powerful devas also pray to you and worship and serve you. Just like kings of small neighbouring kingdoms give taxes to the emperor out of fear, the Devās fear you and respect and worship you.

10.87.29: "Hé ever-liberated Being! When you link yourself with Māya Devi, i.e. your illusory power, different Jīvās dissolved in you come out, and receive movable or immovable bodies in accordance with their previous karmas. You who are supreme, magnanimous and real, are not altered in any way. Jīvās get high or lowly births depending on the karmas done by them previously. What transformation can happen to you, who are above mind, intellect and senses, and are beyond any partiality? There can and never will be anyone like you.

10.87.30: "Hé Immortal One! Though Jīvās are part of you, they are not infinite, complete or immortal like you. This is because if you are the same as Jīvās, there will be two entities. When there is duality, there is difference. The truth is that though God and Jīvās are the same, they remain different as long as objects are there. The ignorant are not aware of this fact.

10.87.31: "It is when Prakṛti and Puruṣa unite that Jīvās are formed. This is like the formation of short lived bubbles as a result of union of air with water. Everything later dissolves in you, the Supreme Being. This can be compared to nectar from many flowers being present in honey or water from various rivers in the ocean.

10.87.32: "The wise, who know that birth and death are illusions, and that thinking otherwise is the cause of pain, take refuge in you. Such people surrender themselves to you, who control time, the cycle of years comprising winter, summer and monsoon as effortlessly as moving an eyebrow. Those who are ignorant of this truth are always afraid of death.

10.87.33: "Some do not worship God as per the instructions of noble preceptors and are not capable of conquering their minds through controlling their senses, and are not able to break free mentally from worldly pleasures. Their attempts to cross the ocean of worldly life, without help from proper preceptors, will be extremely difficult, like sailing in a ship without a captain.

10.87.34: "Of what use is a home, family, gold, land, body, and life to someone who has not taken refuge in you – you, the essence of everything? One can never get the pleasure that he gets when he is approaching you, the nectar of life, from illusory materialistic pursuits. How can worldly pleasures, devoid of any essence, make people happy?

10.87.35: "Ṛṣis, who have given up all attachment to worldly objects, are never arrogant. Even contact with the water used to wash their feet is sufficient to rinse away anybody's sins. Such Ṛṣis have left their homes for ever and live in sanctified hermitages built near sacred rivers, meditating constantly on the feet of the Supreme Lord.

10.87.36: "Brahman is real. So a doubt may arise that how the virtual universe can originate from real Brahman. However, this logic is not applicable in all situations, at all times. Anything that is born out of something need not be that thing. Those who are engrossed in karmās have no time to reflect upon the ultimate truth. They remain ignorant and believe the universe to be real.

10.87.37: "This universe which comprises only names and forms was non-existent before creation in the past and will be so after dissolution in the future. Therefore, it does not exist in the present too, in the middle. It only appears to be real. Gold ornaments like bangles and ear rings are just names and forms; they exist in gold. Similarly, pots and pans are names and forms. They already exist in the earth out of which they are made. In the same way, everything in the universe is just a name and form. Those who mistake the universe to be true are ignorant.

10.87.38: "Jīvan becomes a slave to Māya due to ignorance. Believing the body and sense organs to be real, and considering their actions to be his own, he loses all peace of mind and misses real happiness. On the other hand, like a snake moulting its skin away, you, who are all bliss, shed away all things virtual. And the wise worship you, you who possess the eight infinite prosperities.

10.87.39: "Hé Lord! For those ascetics, who in spite of looking like ones, have not removed desires from their hearts and have neither achieved purity of mind nor realized God present in their own hearts, God is unattainable – like a jewel hidden in their bosom. Yogis also, if they run after sensual pleasures, do not find true happiness in this world or the other.

10.87.40: "Hé seat of all good qualities! Those who know you do not see joy or grief bestowed by you in whatever happens to them on account of their own past karmas; they only see your greatness in everything. They do not experience any positive or negative feelings despite whatever happens to them, unlike the ones who give importance to their bodies. This is because they have shed their ego. As they are always conscious of you through singing or listening to your glory, you grant them ultimate liberation.

10.87.41: "You are infinite in every aspect. Even devas are not aware of your infinite nature. Like specks of dust in the sky, infinite universes revolve within you. We the Śrutis reject everything else and are entirely merged in you."

Here, Śrutigīta ends. Maharṣi Nārāyana then told Nārada:

10.87.42: "The sages who were satisfied with this explanation thanked and saluted Maharṣi Sanandana.

10.87.43: "The essence of karma and Jñāna as presented in the Vedās, Purāṇās, and Upaniṣads were well explained by Maharṣi Sanandana in this Brahmasatram.

10.87.44: "Oh son of Brahma! You have grasped the Śrutigīta in its entirety. Pass on this knowledge to all during your travels."

Śuka Brahmarṣi now concluded his answer to King Parīkṣit in the next five verses (45-49) thus: "Hé King! Sage Nārada, who had listened to Maharṣi Nārāyana, the first Ṛṣi, in rapt attention, bowed before him and his illustrated disciples. Then he offered salutations to Sri Kṛṣna, always immersed in Brahmānanda, and thereafter went to the hermitage of Veda Vyāsa, my father. He then told my father in detail whatever he had heard from Maharṣi Nārāyana. This is how I came to hear Śruti Gīta. Your question was how the Śrutis (Vedās) explain Brahman. Now you know the answer."

In the last verse of this chapter, i.e. 10.87.50, the Brahmarṣi summarised Śruti Gīta for the benefit of King Parīkṣit, so that there was no doubt left in the king's mind about the real nature of Brahman.

CHAPTER 10

MAHIṢIGĪTA

Thousands of years ago, Vidarbha (in present day Maharashtra) was ruled by King Bhīṣmaka. Of his six children, Rukmiṇi was the youngest and his only daughter. The beautiful princess loved Kṛṣṇa, who loved her too. Finally, they got married. Rukmiṇi was thus the first wife of Kṛṣṇa. Later, he married seven other women, including Satyabhāma. Thus, Kṛṣṇa had eight wives now. Peace prevailed everywhere in Dwāraka, under the reign of Kṛṣṇa.

Those days, an asura by name Narakāsura became more and more powerful by defeating one king after another. He imprisoned the daughters of all those vanquished kings. There were sixteen thousand and one hundred princesses in his captivity. He then went to the devaloka and troubled the Devās in umpteen ways.

Devendra related all these atrocities of Narakāsura to Kṛṣṇa. Without any delay, Kṛṣṇa, along with warrior wife Satyabhāma, started off to the invincible fort of Narakāsura in far away Prāgjyothiṣa (in present day Assam).

Overcoming various obstacles like fire, water, hillocks etc surrounding the main fort on all sides, they entered the fort. In the terrible fight that ensued, Kṛṣṇa killed Narakāsura and set all the princesses free. He thought of sending them back to their own respective countries, but all the princesses wanted to marry the heroic Kṛṣṇa! So he sent them all to Dwāraka.

After paying a visit to Indra, when they reached Dwāraka, people gave Kṛṣṇa and Satyabhāma a rousing welcome. The sixteen thousand and one hundred princesses were waiting for the Lord. He married them all at the same time, taking the same number of forms himself! Thus Śrī Kṛṣṇa had sixteen thousand one hundred and eight wives. They all lived in different palaces in Dwāraka, and Kṛṣṇa was with all of them at the same time!

While residing in opulent Dwāraka with his queens, he mesmerised their hearts with charming gestures, tender words and slanting glances. All the queens loved him so intensely that he was all in all for them; they were absorbed entirely in his thoughts. The mystical attraction of the queens to Kṛṣṇa was so overwhelming that they saw their own mood reflected in everyone and everything else.

Ten ślokas of the last and ninetieth chapter of the tenth canto express the ecstatic mood of the queens of Kṛṣṇa. These are together called the Mahisigita, or the Song of the Queens. Here, the queens speak to various creatures of nature, like birds, the ocean, the moon, a cloud, a mountain, a river, and so on – telling them how much they love Kṛṣṇa.

10.90.15: "Hé Kurari (*fish-eating bird*), you are not sleeping and are crying loudly. The Lord is sleeping, why do you want to disturb him? Or, maybe you are also perturbed by the bewitching smile of the lotus-eyed, and are keeping awake like us, unable to sleep.

10.90.16: "Hé Chakravaki (*Ruddy Goose*), you are also crying loudly. Is it that your husband is away and you have closed your eyes? Like us, do you want to place on your head the garland worn on the Lord's feet?

10.90.17: "Hé Ocean! You never sleep and roar loudly. Is it because Mukundan has stolen your gems like the Kaustubha, just like he has stolen our knick-knacks while playing with us?

10.90.18: "Oh Moon! You are silent, maybe because you get dwindled in size every fortnight, and during such times, you are unable to remove the darkness of nights. Or is it because you were expecting to see Mukundan, who has forgotten his promise to us of coming out at night?

10.90.19: "Hé soft and fragrant breeze blowing from sandalwood forests! What good have we done to you, in return for which you are bringing us back to our senses, after we became numb by the glances of Govinda?

10.90.20: "Hé cloud! You are certainly a close friend of the King of the Yādavās. Like us, you meditate upon the one decorated with the Śrīvatsam mark on his chest. Feeling dejected when you cannot see him, you think of him and shed tears of sorrow, forming the rain.

10.90.21: "Oh pleasant-voiced Koel! You coo sweetly like Kṛṣṇa, making us happy, for we often mistake you for him and then decide to go on living. Thus, your words are like Mṛtasanjīvika which make dead people alive. Tell us what we should do for you.

10.90.22: "Hé intelligent mountain! You neither move nor talk. You are all the time thinking. Do you wish the son of Vasudeva to place his feet on your peak? Alas, you are also grieving like us.

10.90.23: "Hé friends! As we cannot at present rejoice in the loving glances of Madhupati, we are torn apart in grief and have become lean and thin and have lost the glow on our faces. The condition of this dry river is just like that of ours. In this summer, they are not getting any water and have become very narrow.

10.90.24: "Hé swan! Have you arrived here safely? Please sit down and drink some milk. We know that you are Kṛṣṇa's messenger. Tell us about him. Is he well? Does he remember what he had told us earlier? His affection is not stable. Bring him to us alone, without Lakṣmi. Is she the only woman whose adoration for him is everlasting?

Here, this gīta, sung by the queens (Mahishis) of Kṛṣṇa, ends. Due to such undiluted love for Kṛṣṇa, who is the master of all gods, his queens attain mokṣa when the time comes. Life was a continuing penance for these women. They were blessed to lead such a life, as they had become one with Kṛṣṇa, the master of the Universe.

CHAPTER 11

HAṀSAGĪTA

The latter part of the eleventh canto of the Bhāgavat Purān is mostly in the form of a detailed question-answer session. The one who put the questions was Uddhava. In his last birth, he was the foremost disciple of Devaguru Bṛhaspati, while in this birth he was one of the greatest devotees of Lord Kṛṣna. The one who answered the questions was Kṛṣna himself.

The purpose of Viṣnu's incarnation as Kṛṣna on Earth was over. It was now time for Lord Kṛṣna to leave this world and return to his original abode, the Vaikunṭha. However, before doing that, he knew that his entire race must end too. His people had become powerful due to his presence among them. If he ascended Heaven leaving them behind, they were sure to become autocratic. Kṛṣna did not want this to happen. As nobody else could destroy them, it was imperative that they would quarrel among themselves and destroy each other. Ultimately, this was what exactly took place.

Seeing all this, Uddhava was perturbed. "What is all this, O Lord? What is going to happen? I am sure that you are also leaving the earth for good. O Bhagvān, please do not leave me and go away! How can I live without you? Please take me to wherever you are going!"

In this way, Uddhava cried aloud and pleaded piteously with Kṛṣna.

Kṛṣna was touched by Uddhava's simplicity and devotion. Lovingly, he told his devotee: "What you have guessed is right, my friend. The purpose of my incarnation is now over. After the end of the Yādava race, I will leave this Earth and go away too. Dwāraka is destined to go down in to the depths of the sea on the seventh day from today. Kaliyuga will begin on Earth the moment I leave it. However, my dear Uddhava, you need not worry. You are my true devotee. I shall tell you what to do."

And thus started the lengthy dialogue between the Lord and Uddhava. This advice in its entirety is known as Uddhavagīta. Within this, there are three separate Gītās – Hamsagīta, Bhikṣugīta, and Ailagīta. All the three are in the form of informative stories as said by the Lord to Uddhava.

In the course of the continuing dialogue, Uddhava said, "Hé Kṛṣna, people who are desirous of mokṣa are aware of the fact that objects that augment sensual pleasures are to be shunned; yet they fall for the same. Why is it so?"

Lord Kṛṣna replied, "When rājasik thoughts increase in the mind, people decide that they must enjoy materialistic pleasures. Though they know that materialism is dangerous, rājasik thoughts dominate and dim this knowledge. As a result, human beings engage in activities that lead to misery. Satvaguṇa increases dharma, which destroys rajas and tamas and thereby adharma.

"At least some people succeed in reducing their desires, and become sātvik. Those who find it hard to do so can try to control their mind through yoga. Once I had explained the intricacies of yoga and its practice to Sage Sanaka and others."

On hearing this, Uddhava wished to know the details of what Kṛṣna had told them. Lord Kṛṣna then described in detail the events related to the whole incident. He said:

"Once, the four sons of Lord Brahma—Sages Sanaka, Sananda (Sanandana), Sanātana and Sanalkumāra—approached their father and requested him to explain how to separate mind from desires. Though Lord Brahma is an enlightened soul, as he is always engaged in the act of creation, he could not find a suitable answer to this question. So he thought of me and immediately I presented myself before him in the form of a swan. On seeing me, he knew that it was I, for I would be able to explain how to separate mind from desires, just as a swan can separate milk from water. Sanaka and his brothers also somehow felt that reverence was due to me.

"Taking their father's permission, they began conversing with me. In the beginning, they asked me, 'Who are you?' And I began my discourse. Hé Uddhava, I shall now tell you what I told them that day. Listen carefully".

All that the Lord told Uddhava at this juncture is called Haṁsagīta. It is called so as the Lord was relating to Uddhava all that he, in the form of a haṁsaṁ (swan) had told Rishi Sanaka and his brothers. Hamsagīta comprises nineteen ślokās—from verse twenty-two to verse forty—of the thirteenth chapter of the eleventh canto of Śrīmad Bhāgavatam.

11.13.22: "Hé Brāhmins (sages)! How does your question make sense, when soul has no plurality? If you mean my soul, it is not different from your souls. Or do you mean my body? Without knowing this, how can I answer your question?

11.13.23: "If you mean the body, all bodies are made of the five elements. So all bodies are in effect one and the same. Therefore your speech, starting with this question, is quite meaningless.

11.13.24: "I am all that, all that is comprehended with the mind, or words or eyes or any other sense organ. Understand, using your intellect, that there is nothing different or separate from me.

11.13.25: "Hé sons! The mind enters Guṇās, i.e. sātvik, rājasik and tāmasik qualities, and qualities enter the mind. The resultant product of union of the mind and the qualities is Jīvan, which is part of Brahma, i.e. me.

11.13.26: "By promoting thought of Guṇās, the mind enters into them. Similarly, Guṇās also increase in intensity as they become fixed on the mind. In this way, Guṇās and the mind feed each other. However, when one realizes that he is neither of these, only then will he come to understand his true nature.

11.13.27: "The three states of wakefulness, sleep, and dreamless deep sleep (jāgṛt, swapn and suṣupti) are caused by sātvik, rājasik and tāmasik Guṇās respectively. These are the workings of the intellect. But Jīva is present in and is witness to all these three states.

11.13.28: "Guṇās are the basis of the three states of life. One should realize that the fourth state, i.e. turīya, is independent of the three basic states. I am this state; those who remain fixed in this state, i.e. me, will be able to give up all relationships with the world.

11.13.29: "It is because of ego that one thinks that his actions are decided by his intellect. One who has shed his ego exists in me who is witness to the three states, and gives up all material thoughts.

11.13.30: "Till he becomes enlightened, an ignorant person is asleep, though he is awake. His state is like being awake in a dream. In other words, a sleeping man believes his dream to be real. On waking up, he realizes that it was all a dream. Similarly, as long as one is ignorant, he does not realize the truth.

11.13.31: "Everything seems to exist in plurality (like karmās, consequences of karmās etc.); but these are not applicable to ātma, the soul. When one realizes that the soul is one, this ignorance disappears like how a dream vanishes when the dreaming person wakes up.

11.13.32: "When awake, one experiences worldly objects through sense organs; when asleep, he experiences them in dreams; and when in deep sleep, dissolves everything in himself. This controller of all senses, this witness to everything, is the soul and it is single.

11.13.33: "Understand by reasoning that the three states caused by the three Guṇās are an illusion produced by me. Realize this truth and cut off the source of all your doubts with the help of the sharp sword which is this knowledge, and pray to me who exists in your heart.

11.13.34: "What is seen is only an illusion, a dream, created by the mind; it is a misconception that this world is real. If a piece of firewood burning at one end is rotated, the fire looks circular, though it is present only at the tip of the burning stick. Similarly, the universe is just an imagination of the mind that exists in three states because of the three Guṇās.

11.13.35: "Therefore, withdraw your mind from the universe, and enjoy the resultant bliss within. Do not crave for materialistic objects, perform karmas but without desiring for results, and keep calm at all times. In case you see the world as real at times, the knowledge that it is not real will help in realizing its dream-like nature. Thus, a wise person will experience his body, but he will know that it is not real. This knowledge will always remain with him.

11.13.36: "An enlightened person (a siddha) does not see whether a mortal body is sitting or standing (meaning doing any work). This is because he knows that the body lives as long as its karmas are exhausted, a new body will be formed again, to exhaust newly acquired karmas. A siddha knows that the real he is the soul while an ignorant person believes that he is his body and that the body is real.

11.13.37: "There is no doubt that the body exists as long as karmas which caused its birth exist; once these karmas are exhausted, the body falls. As a siddha knows that his body is a dream, he is in a state of samādhi at all times. Hence, after the fall of his body, he is not born again.

11.13.38: "Hé Brāhmins! I have now imparted to you the knowledge hidden in Sāṁkhya and Yoga. Know that I, who have come here to give this dhārmik advice to you, am none other than Viṣṇu.

11.13.39: "Oh noble Brahmaṇās, I am that destination to reach which different people go along different paths like yoga, sāṁkhya, dharma (righteousness), satya (honesty), tapasya (penance), saṁpatti (prosperity), kīrti (fame), dama (controlling senses) etc.

11.13.40: "I am without guṇa and without dependence on anyone or anything. I am the friend of all, the seat of love and the soul. Composure and dispassion, which are not products of the three Guṇās, depend on me and worship me."

Here, the Haṁsagīta ends.

In 11.13.41, Lord Sri Kṛṣna concludes telling this story to Uddhava thus: "In this way, I cleared all the doubts of Sages Sanaka and his brothers. They thanked and praised me with deep devotion, and sang my glory."

In 11.13.42, he continues: "Accepting their reverent salutations, in the presence of Lord Brahma, I left the place and reached my abode".

The thirteenth chapter of the eleventh canto of Śrīmad Bhāgavatam ends here, with this forty second verse.

CHAPTER 12

BHIKṢUGĪTA

The eleventh canto of the Bhāgavat Purāna comprises mostly the advice given by Lord Kṛṣna to his faithful friend and devotee Uddhava. "Give up everything you considered yours till now; see me in everything and practise self-realisation; and you will certainly attain mokṣa", said the Lord.

But Uddhava wanted to know in detail how he could do this. So Lord Kṛṣna began his explanations by giving suitable instructions to Uddhava. He also cited certain stories to prove his point. One of these stories was that of a Bhikṣu (an ascetic).

Uddhava had a question. "O Lord, you have always said that arrogance must be shunned if one has to attain mokṣa. As long as one is aware of and takes pride in his physical form, he also has to suffer humiliations afflicted upon his body and mind. How must one react to such insults?"

It was in reply to this question that Lord Kṛṣna narrated to him the story of the Bhikṣu who was once a householder. The Lord said:

11.23.4-27: "I shall tell you a story to prove my point. Listen attentively. It is about a Sanyāsi who was insulted by all, owing to his own past karmas, and how he overcame them all. As a householder, this Brāhmin living in Avanti was a wealthy farmer, also with various businesses. He was greedy, miserly, and short tempered, and did not treat his family members or others well. He did not spend anything for charity, nor did he please any god. Over time, he became a pauper due to many reasons. None cared for him.

"By old age, he was all alone. Distressed to the core, he analysed profoundly his past life and deeds, and realized that he had wasted precious years in amassing wealth for himself, and did not do anything for the sake of others. Greed had ruined him. He understood that creating and maintaining wealth are equally strenuous, leading to misery in the end. Affluence gives rise to many bad qualities like dishonesty, arrogance, duplicity, anger, unhealthy competition, discrimination, thoughtlessness, distrust, intolerance, yearning for others' wealth etc.

"He understood how family and friends neglect one who has become poor. Even after being born as a human being, and that as a Brāhmin, he had shunned piety and wasted his life desirous of riches and the pleasures that could be bought with it. He was sure he would rot in hell. Of what use was his working hard to be rich."

Kṛṣṇa then related to Uddhava how the old Brāhmin found out the ultimate truth thorough introspection. The Brāhmin thought to himself:

11.23.28-30: "I am sure Lord Hari is pleased with me, for all those who are in my situation, dispassion is the ultimate solution, and I have realized it now. So I will try to remain absorbed in my inner consciousness as long as I live. May the gods bless me."

Kṛṣṇa continued:

11.23.31-42: "With this firm determination, the Brāhmin castoff the thoughts of 'I', 'me' and 'mine' completely, and became an ascetic. Controlling his mind and senses, he roamed about in faraway places begging for alms from unknown people. Wicked people insulted this old man in unclean attire in many ways. Approaching the muni sitting peacefully on the riverbank, about to have his food received in alms, some snatched away his vessel of food, others his kamanḍulu with drinking water; some others took away his yogadanḍu, japamāla, sittig mat, bark clothing etc. To make fun of him, some pretended to give these articles back to him, and when he extended his hand to collect them, jeered at him and walked away, without returning his meagre possessions. Some evil-minded men spat or even urinated on his head. Some compelled the muni to talk. But when he remained silent, they beat him. Shouting loudly that he was a thief in disguise, some bound him with ropes and accused him of being a fraud, bent upon cheating people. The wrong-doers as well as the onlookers laughed loudly at his helplessness.

"The old man however was least affected by any of these. He bore them all and remained calm as he had controlled his mind. He thought that all this was the result of his bad karmas. Full of courage resulting from his satvaguṇa, he sang the following song."

This song in sixteen verses is famous as 'Bhikṣugīta.' It is one of the most enlightening parts of Kṛṣna's advice to Uddhava. The Brāhmin said:

11.23.43: "This world is not the cause of my joys and sorrows. It is not the gods, the people, the planets, my own deeds or time either. I say that the real cause of joys and sorrows is the mind, which makes the whole universe revolve. It is in the mind that happiness and grief are experienced.

11.23.44: "Mind has good and bad qualities. From these qualities, white and black and red (sātvik, tāmasik and rājasik) thoughts originate. Based on the proportions of these, corresponding deeds are done. This results in the joys and sorrows of all creatures.

11.23.45: "Even when the mind is good and working well, the soul has no worldly connection. It is because of ignorance that it appears that the Jīvātma is bound by worldly matters. Even though Paramātma controls the mind which is engaged in various activities, worldly matters do not affect it, as it possesses vidya, i.e. true knowledge. At the same time, the ignorant believe that mind is of utmost importance and become its slaves.

11.23.46: "Good acts like charity, doing one's duties, cleanliness, non-violence, thirst for gaining knowledge, fasting for good purposes etc. help one to conquer his mind. This is in effect yoga itself, which will ultimately lead to mokṣa.

11.23.47: "If one has total peace of mind, and has firm belief in the immortality of his soul, he need not even practise charity. But if on account of never ending desires, one's mind does not work properly, then also good deeds like charity are of no use to him because the purpose of doing good deeds is to get mental peace.

11.23.48: "Senses and their controlling deities obey mind; but the mind does not obey them. Mind is thus all powerful. Whoever has control over such powerful mind is noble and fit to be worshipped by even devas.

11.23.49: "Some unthinking people, instead of conquering the mind which works with immense speed and is extremely difficult to surmount, fight with friends and relatives and enemies, and even those who are indifferent to them.

11.23.50: "Some people have no wisdom; they cannot differentiate the real from the unreal. Such people believe that this body is real and it possesses many faculties. They think, "I am this body; that body is someone else", and so on and so forth. In this way, they wander in the darkness of ignorance and get distressed.

11.23.51: "Mind is the cause of all joys and sorrows. It is wrong to blame others for that. The soul carries out no actions. So the cause of joys and sorrows is not the soul. This means that the body is the doer and experiencer of all deeds. What is the meaning in blaming others if one bites his tongue with his own teeth?

11.23.52: "That the joys and sorrows of people result from God's actions is also not true. This is because the gods themselves will have to face results of their actions. If one organ of a person harms another organ of his own body, how can he blame any of the two?

11.23.53: "If it is the soul that causes joys and sorrows of people, then people will try to get rid of the soul. But this is not done; it is not possible either. The argument that the soul acts in this way due to external influence can also not be supported, because there is nothing other than the soul. Ultimately, no cause can be found for the joys and sorrows of men. This proves that there is nothing like joys and sorrows. So there is no meaning in blaming anybody or anything.

11.23.54: If it is the planetary positions during birth that cause joys and sorrows, how is the soul affected? Soul does not have joys and sorrows. Soul is not born. What is born is the body. It is only the ignorant who think that pain—physical as well as mental—of the body are caused by planets. So at whom can men be angry?

11.23.55: If karma is the cause of joys and sorrows, so be it. Soul is not affected. The body is mortal; so it will have karmas and their results as long as the body is alive. However, the soul which is knowledge itself does not perform any karma. Then at whom can a person be angry?

11.23.56: "Suppose joys and sorrows are caused by good and bad times. However, soul is not affected by time. Time is everywhere and is indivisible; it is universe itself. Sparks of fire do not get heated up by fire; nor are flakes of snow made any cooler by the snow. This shows that Paramātma is beyond dualities and so experiences neither joy nor sorrow. So any person cannot direct his anger towards anything or anyone.

11.23.57: "The soul is not related to joys or sorrows in any situation, at any place or time. It is not affected by anyone or anything. It is only the ego that creates dichotomies like happiness and grief, where none exists. One who knows this fact is never afraid of the Pancabhūtās.

11.23.58: "Sages of the past were able to gain true knowledge by meditating on the Supreme Being. I too will cross the vast sea of ignorance by worshipping the feet of Lord Mahāviṣnu."

Here, Bhikṣugīta ends. Concluding the story, Sri Kṛṣna says:

11.23.59: "The Bhikṣu who had lost everything, discarded all his sorrows through detaching himself from the materialistic world, and took to sanyās. In spite of being insulted by the wicked, he did not deviate from his morals and travelled far and wide singing this Bhikṣugīta.

11.23.60: "Jīvan gets joys and sorrows only through imagination of the mind. The assumption that the world comprises friends, enemies and the neutral is caused by lack of knowledge of the Supreme Being and the fact that there is no real existence of the universe.

11.23.61: "Therefore, dear disciple, fix your intellect on me. Overcoming joys and sorrows is by conquering the mind and fixing one's intellect on me. This is the essential principle of yoga.

11.23.62: "Those who recite for others or hear from others this Bhikṣugīta, understand its meaning clearly, will be able to triumph over their mind and will not be affected by the dualities of joys and sorrows."

The twenty third chapter of the eleventh canto of Śrīmad Bhāgavat Purān ends here.

The gist of the bhikṣu's story is that when one has controlled his mind, he is not affected by the words or actions of anyone. There is nothing that such a man cannot achieve. He is not scared of anything – not even death. He knows that just like dreams appear to be real when one is asleep, the whole world seems to be real as long as one is ignorant. When he gains true knowledge, he realises that the whole world is actually virtual. Nothing else exists except the Supreme Being.

Those who listen to Bhikṣugīta with full attention and try to fix their minds in the Supreme Being will be able to face any situation in life.

CHAPTER 13

AILAGĪTA

A king named Satyavrata used to rule the present day South India. He was a very pious king and used to worship Lord Viṣṇu without fail. After the great deluge, he was born as Vaivasvata Manu, who later married Śraddhā Devi. Even after many years, thcy did not have a child. Therefore, Manu organized a yāga for begetting a son. However, his wife had told the rishis beforehand to perform the rituals in such a way that a daughter would be born to her. The rishis did accordingly. Thus a baby girl was born. She was named Ila.

Soon Manu went to Maharṣi Vasiṣṭha and asked him, "I had prayed for a son during the yāga. How come my prayer wasn't answered?"

The maharṣi sat with eyes closed for a while. By his spiritual powers, he found out the reason and disclosed the same to Manu. Seeing the latter's disappointment, Vasiṣṭha prayed to Nārāyana to change Ila into a boy. The Lord obliged the sage. Ila became a boy. He was named Sudyumna.

Once, Sudyumna went hunting in the forest. On entering a particular resort by chance, he suddenly became a maiden! This was because of a spell cast on the place by Lord Śiva. Long ago, some sages had entered this resort of Śiva and Pārvati, intruding into their privacy. Then Lord Śiva had said, "From now on, any man who enters this place will become a woman."

Thus Sudyumna became Ila again! Budha, the God of Planet Mercury, fell in love with her and married her. Soon, a son was born to them. He was named Purūravas. He had another name, Aila, as he was the son of Ila.

Purūravas grew into a very handsome and valorous prince. He was very affectionate by nature and was loved by all. Coming to know of his charisma and good qualities from Sage Nārada, Urvaśi, the apsara maiden, came down to Earth to see him. The king was equally attracted by Urvaśi's charm. Without delay, he proposed to her.

Urvaśi now set a condition. She said: "I have two pet goats. They always live with me. If you promise to have them with you and look after them yourself, I shall marry you!"

The king, though noble and intelligent, was blinded by love. He agreed to Urvaśi's condition and married her. From that day, the king kept the goats in his room and took them out for grazing and saw to it that they were comfortable!

In this way, days went by. In the meantime, not finding Urvaśi in the Devaloka, Indra sent messengers everywhere to search for her. Some of them found out her whereabouts. They took the goats away. Urvaśi now had to return to Indra.

King Purūravas was heartbroken. He followed her to Devaloka and requested her to come back to Earth. Taking pity on the king, the apsara agreed to come to Earth for one day every year.

Purūravas had to be content with Urvaśi's decision. He came back and spent his days in sadness, ever waiting for the day Urvaśi would come to the earth. In this way, years passed by. Finally, the king realized how foolish he had been for so many years.

After realising his mistakes, King Purūravas determined to conquer his senses. What he told himself at that time is called 'Ailagīta'. His repentance is presented in eight verses (11.26.7-

14), and his determination in ten verses (11.26.15-24), totalling eighteen.

Lord Kṛṣna gave an introduction to this gīta to Uddhava in three verses.

11.26.4: "Purūravas was a famous emperor; his grief was great at separation from Urvaśi. Later, on becoming dispassionate, his grief evaporated and he sang this song.

11.26.5: "When Urvaśi had left him, he had run after her, crying loudly and beseeching her to come back, forgetting the fact that he was stark naked at the time and that he was an emperor.

11.26.6: "Attracted by Urvaśi and enslaved by lust, he had no idea how many days and nights he had spent in her company, longing for sensual pleasures."

Ailagīta begins here. On getting back his wisdom, Purūravas said with deep remorse:

11.26.7: "I had become a slave to the wicked Kāma; so I did not know that ensnared by Urvaśi, I was wasting my life. How immersed in ignorance I was.

11.26.8: "I did not notice the sun rising or setting. Entranced by her, alas, I did not realize that days were flying past.

11.26.9: "I am the noblest of kings. I am an emperor. Yet I was behaving like a pet deer at the hands of a woman. Alas, it is unbelievable how I forgot everything.

11.26.10: "I ran after her crying pitiably, stark naked like a mad man, even after knowing that she cared little for me or my empire.

11.26.11: "Like a donkey, I followed her even after being kicked by her. Where did my nobility, strength and knowledge disappear?

11.26.12: "Of what use is one's education, penance, expertise in vedās, solitary living, speech control, or even sanyās, if his heart is stolen by women?

11.26.13: "I who do not know how to conduct myself; I who pretend to be learned though I am a fool, must be condemned.

Despite achieving nobility and closeness to God, I was won over by women; so I rightly deserve censure.

11.26.14: "I have been enjoying Urvaśi's intoxicating kisses for many years. My craving for lust was never satiated. It only grew more and more, like a fire in which ghee is poured.

11.26.15: "Only God, who is ever present in me, and who has conquered senses can pull my mind away from her, who has stolen my heart.

11.26.16: "Even though she awakened lust in me, Urvaśi did give me the right advice. She told me not to waste my life in her company. Despite all this, my ignorance did not disappear. I am not intelligent. I did not conquer my senses.

11.26.17: "I am to blame and not she, for I was the one who mistook a rope for a snake. What is the fault of the rope in this? I was not able to vanquish my passion for lust. It is all my fault.

11.26.18: "The body is in fact unclean and foul smelling; if anyone feels that it is fragrant, it is sheer illusion.

11.26.19: "Pride in this body is due to ignorance. Whose is this body – is it one's parents as they are the cause of this body, or is it the wife's as she claims the person to be her husband? Does the body belong to the superior as one has to obey him? Does this body belong to the fire as the fire claims it after death? Or does it belong to the dogs or vultures that may tear it up and eat it after death? Is it one's own as the claimant to the effects of the karmās done by it is the Jīvan? Nothing is certain.

11.26.20: "Ignorant men are attracted by women's bodies, which will be destroyed sooner or later. Such men are mistakenly enticed by their charming face, beautiful features, and enchanting smile.

11.26.21: "Some find pleasure in bodies made of skin, flesh, blood, nerves, fat, bones and marrow and which hold waste materials like urine and faeces. What difference is there between such people and the lowly worms?

11.26.22: "The mind becomes turbulent when sense organs respond to senses. This does not happen by any other means.

Therefore, men and women who know this truth do not keep the company of lovers.

11.26.23: "The mind does not crave for unseen or unheard objects. Such objects are therefore not the cause of tempestuous minds. Those who do not run after attractive objects, even if seen or heard, have truly controlled their sense organs. Such people remain calm.

11.26.24: "In short, it is not good for men to keep the company of women, or other men attracted by women. Even knowledgeable men cannot be sure of having controlled their sense organs and mind. Winning over them is therefore impossible for the ignorant like me. I must at least try to do that."

In 11.26.25, Lord Śrī Kṛṣna tells Uddhava that in this way, Emperor Purūravas concluded singing the Ailagīta. True knowledge dawned on him. Desires burnt away, he distanced himself mentally from Urvaśi and her world. Conquering his mind and sense organs, he meditated on me and finally became one with me. Śrī Kṛṣna thus impressed upon Uddhava on what was to be done to attain mokṣa.

CHAPTER 14

UDDHAVAGĪTA

As mentioned in Chapter 11, a large part of the eleventh canto of the Bhāgavat Purāna comprises the advice given by Lord Kṛṣna to Uddhava, which in the whole is referred to as Uddhavagīta. Hamsagīta, Bhikṣugīta, and Ailagīta, described in the eleventh, twelfth, and thirteenth chapters respectively, are parts of Uddhavagīta. Therefore the parts not covered in these three Gītās are dealt with here, in this fourteenth chapter.

One day, all the Devās including Lord Brahma and Lord Śiva and all other celestials appeared in the sky over Kṛṣna's palace in Dwāraka. Hearing their prayers, Kṛṣna came out, blessed them all and enquired the purpose of their visit.

"Long ago, you took birth on this earth, as per our request, O Lord," began the creator, "and you have fulfilled all our wishes and much more. The purpose of your incarnation is over, Bhagvān. Please return to Vaikuntha. Moreover, you have turned a hundred and twenty five, O Lord, and so also, it is time to leave the earth. There is nothing that you do not know of; still it is our duty to remind you. On the way to Vaikuntha, please come to my abode also."

Kṛṣna replied: "What you say is absolutely true. It is time I go back to Vaikuntha. There are two more deeds left for me to do on this earth. One is the destruction of my own race. My people have become powerful due to my presence among them. If I depart leaving them behind, they will become autocratic. The other important work that I have to do while still here is to leave some spiritual advice with mankind in the form of teachings to Uddhava. Both these will be accomplished very soon. After that, I shall return to Vaikuntha, through Brahmaloka."

The Devās prostrated before Kṛṣna, thanked him and returned to their respective abodes.

Bad omens first appeared in Dwāraka the day Kṛṣna's son Sāmba and his friends were cursed by some venerable rishis, whom they had insulted. Details of how they incurred this curse are given in the first chapter of the eleventh canto. On King Parīkṣit's request, Maharṣi Śuka had elaborated the whole incident.

One day, Shree Kṛṣṇa invited some eminent Maharṣis like Viśvāmitra, Bhṛgu, Kaṇva, Vasiṣtha, Vāmadeva, Nārada, Kaśyapa, Durvāsa, Angiras, Atri, Asita etc. to Dwāraka to perform certain rituals for the welfare of the entire populace. After the completion of the rituals, he thanked them and bade them farewell.

While the sages were going back, a group of young Yādava men went after them. One of them incited his friends to test the Ṛṣis for their mystical powers. Accordingly, Sāmban, son of Kṛṣṇa and Jāmbavati, was dressed as a pregnant woman. Then, with affected humility, they approached the Ṛṣis and asked them whether the pregnant woman's baby would be a boy or a girl.

The Ṛṣis understood with their divine insight that the men were playing a dirty prank on them. Annoyed greatly, they replied that the woman would give birth to neither a boy nor a girl, but an iron pestle which would destroy their entire race.

When the terrified young men hurriedly undressed Sāmban, they saw a small piece of iron sticking to his thigh. Frightened to the core, they ran to King Ugrasena and reported the matter to him. The king advised them to file the piece of iron into fine powder and put it in the ocean.

The Yādava youths followed this advice. Nonetheless, a small piece was left after filing the iron pestle for a long time. They threw it into the ocean along with the powder. By chance, a fish ate that piece of iron. Later, a hunter named Jara caught this fish. On cutting it open, he saw the piece of iron inside. He sharpened it and fixed it to the tip of one of his arrows for future use. In the meantime, the fine iron dust in the ocean was washed ashore. These were absorbed by the roots of some wild grasses growing nearby. The young men knew nothing about all this and spent their days in happy abandon.

Kṛṣṇa the all-knowing thought: "The Yādavās have reached the height of their prosperity. Now it is time for their downfall. This is the time for action. The enlightened will not be affected by rise or fall."

Day by day, evil omens increased in number and intensity in Dwāraka. The alarmed citizens of the city sought Kṛṣna's advice. The Lord said: "Living here is not desirable any longer. Let us go to holy Prabhāsa at the sea coast."

Śrī Śuka tells King Parīkṣit at this point:

11.6.40-42: "O noble King! The Yādavās, thus instructed by Kṛṣṇa, quickly made all necessary preparations. Hearing Kṛṣṇa's words and seeing and hearing all the commotion, Uddhava was distraught. He went to Kṛṣṇa in solitude. He prostrated himself before the Lord and began conveying his fears to him."

Uddhavagīta commences from here, with Uddhava addressing Lord Kṛṣṇa thus:

11.6.43-50: "O Īśwara of all gods, you are omniscient; yet you have not taken any measure to nullify the sages' curse that has fallen upon the Yādavās. It looks to me as if the whole Yādava race is about to be destroyed and that you are also leaving the earth for good. O Bhagvān, please do not leave me and go away! I cannot live for even half a second without you. Please take me to wherever you are going.

"Hé Kṛṣṇa! Forgetting their worldly woes, people listen to your deeds with great adoration, love and affection. We, your devotees, live thinking of you at all times. That way, we are able to cross this ocean of worldly existence easily. Great Ṛṣis, living on air, perform severe penance, and Sanyāsis, controlling their senses, live a life of nomads. All of them are unified with you in the end. However, we your devotees, even while living and moving about in this world, feel liberated as we are constantly relishing your caring words and actions, and loving smile and glances."

Narrating the story to King Parīkṣit, Maharṣi Śuka says here:

11.6.51: "In this way, Uddhava pleaded with Kṛṣna. Kṛṣna was touched by Uddhava's simplicity and devotion. Lovingly, he began addressing his devotee."

Here ends the sixth chapter of the eleventh canto. At the beginning of the seventh chapter, Bhagvān Kṛṣṇa said:

11.7.1-12: "What you have guessed is right, my lucky friend. It was as per the request of Brahma and others that I took birth on this earth. The purpose of my incarnation is now over. The Yādava race is nearing its end. I will leave this Earth and go away too. Dwāraka is destined to go down in to the depths of the sea on the seventh day from today. Kaliyuga will begin on the earth the moment I leave it and go away. People will become dishonest and immoral. The world will no longer be a place to your liking. You are my true devotee, so I shall tell you what to do. Give up everything you considered yours till now. Travel around, seeing me in everything.

"Know that whatever is perceived through mind, words, eyes, ears etc. is all mortal and is a product of imagination of the mind; hence all this is pure illusion. One who has not conquered his mind does not realize oneness in the universe; he believes in diversity of creation. Hence he differentiates between karmas of different kinds. Therefore, master your sense organs and mind and see the universe in your soul and your soul in me. No obstacles will appear before a person who is happy in this knowledge and is at peace within. One who has risen above the level of good and evil performs good deeds not for gaining anything; he does not perform evil deeds not out of fear of hell. It is his natural behaviour; that is all. He is a well-wisher of all and knows the truth. As he sees God in all, no danger befalls him after death of the body."

In 11.7.13, Maharṣi Śuka says that the pious Uddhava prostrated before Kṛṣna and requested him to elaborate the topic.

Uddhava said:

11.7.14-18: "Hé Originator and Master of all Yogās! You have told me the method of dispassion for attaining mokṣa. This method is not suitable for the ignorant like me. I am not able to come out of māya. It is not easy for me to give up everything and go away. How can I give up thoughts about me and my people and my things so easily? Please tell me what I should do to develop such a sense of detachment. Subject to your māya, even gods are conscious of their bodies. None can give me the right answer to this question except you."

To this, Lord Śrī Kṛṣna replied fondly:

11.7.19-24: "A person who is introspective, who constantly analyses every fact and thought can understand this truth. Such a person is his own guru and attains mokṣa over time. The intelligent, who have mastered Sāṁkhya and Yoga, clearly see the all comprehensive Ātma which is me. Being born as a human being is a great achievement indeed. Various types of animals, like those with one foot, two feet, three feet, four feet, many feet and some without any feet, have been created. Of all these, two legged human beings are the most intelligent. Only humans have the intelligence to realize the absolute truth and thereby attain mokṣa. To clarify my point, I shall tell you an old story about a dialogue between the great Yadu and a hermit.

11.7.25: "Emperor Yadu, the founder of our Yādava race, once met a yogi. The latter was in fact Maharṣi Dattātreya, who was most handsome, but least bothered about his appearance. The Maharṣi was youthful, as he was free from worries. He was fearless, intelligent, strong, and ever happy."

Yadu asked him:

11.7.26-30: "O wise sage! How is it that you are leading such a happy and carefree life like a child? Usually, humans desire long life, fame and wealth and work for that. However, despite being intelligent, handsome, strong and excellent in oratory, you move about casually like a mad man, not wanting anything. While others are burning in the fire of greed and lust, you like an elephant, are revelling in the cool water of the Ganges. Oh Brahma-Jñāni without any desire, what is the cause of this immense joy in your heart? Kindly enlighten me.

11.27.31: "So saying, Emperor Yadu prostrated before Dattātreya, the Brāhmin sage. The sage answered the question thus.

11.7.32-36: "I have not one, but many gurus. They did not give me any advice; I observed them carefully and learnt many valuable lessons from them. I have twenty four such gurus. They are the earth, air, sky, water, fire, moon, sun, pigeon, python, ocean, moth, beetle, elephant, honey collector, deer, fish, the woman by name Pingala, the bird kapotam (dove), child, girl, blacksmith making arrows, snake, spider and hunter. I shall tell you, Oh son of Yayāti, the lessons I learnt from each of these twenty four teachers.

11.7.37-38: "The earth is all forgiving. She is not moved by anything. Even when treated badly, she remains calm. Thus the earth taught me that one should remain composed and be patient. Mountains contain infinite wealth in them, including trees and rivers and minerals, but all that is for others. I thus learnt selflessness from the mountains on the earth. I must live for others.

11.7.39-41: "Air is everywhere, but it does not adopt the qualities of anything. For example, the air may carry fragrance, but those who know that the fragrance is in the flower, will not think that the air is fragrant. Like air which is not interested in external objects, one must not be attracted by worldly matters. One who has controlled his senses, even while interacting with the world, does not get attached to it. Though all depend on air, air does not depend on anyone or anything. An enlightened yogi is like that.

11.7.42-43: "The sky is everywhere – inside and outside all that is created. Yet it is not joined with anything; nor is it separated from anything. Same is the case with ātma; even when it is inside us, it is also outside us as Brahman. Clouds are not connected to the sky even though they are seen in the sky; similarly, ātma is not affected by the body.

11.7.44: "Water is pure and soft. It cleanses everything which it comes in contact with. We also must purify others who are in our company. A sage, like water, is pure of heart and always helps others. He is soft spoken and loving, and is respected by all.

11.7.45-47: "Fire burns brightly, removing darkness. Similarly, a good sage glowing in his spiritual powers removes the ignorance of others and makes them enlightened. Fire eats whatever it gets; a sage eats whatever he gets in alms too. Fire is pure; similarly, a sage is sinless. Fire burns everything and benefits its maker. In the same way, a sage destroys the sins of those who approach him, thereby helping them. Fire is hidden in wood. Yet it manifests only when lit. Similarly, the ātma is present in the whole universe, though not explicitly seen. Fire has no particular shape; it takes the shape of the thing that is burning. In the same way, ātma is the same though the bodies that contain it are of various shapes. All this I have learnt from Fire.

11.7.48-49: "The size of the moon itself does not increase or decrease, even though the crescent does so. Similarly, time affects only the body, which is born, ages and dies. But this is not the case of the soul – it is neither born nor dies, though the bodies it occupies do so.

11.7.50-51: "The sun takes water from water bodies and gives it out as rain, but it does not claim to be the giver and taker. Similarly, a sage does not take pride in his activities. Moreover, reflections of the sun will be different in different water bodies. That does not mean that the sun has different forms. Seeing this, I have learnt that God is the same in all creatures.

11.7.52-74: "If one gets too much attached to anyone or anything, he will have to suffer intense sorrow. The story of the dove corroborates this fact. Once there lived a dove couple on a tree in a forest. They loved each other passionately and spent all their time in each other's company. Whatever the wife asked for, the husband gave it to her, even if with great difficulty. When the she dove laid eggs, they were exultant and waited eagerly for the eggs to hatch. One after the other, the eggs hatched and beautiful tiny dovelings covered with silky hair peeped out to the great excitement of the father and mother doves. The loving parents enjoyed watching their movements and listening to their melodious tweets. The affection between the parents grew further due to their common love for their children.

"Once, while the parents had flown out to bring food for the chicks, a hunter caught the dovelings in his net. Knowing that the parents would soon return, he waited in hiding. On return, the mother saw her children fluttering in the net, trying their best to escape. The mother was beside herself with grief. Not knowing how to save her children, she also jumped into the net. The father who flew in just then saw the pitiable sight. Unable to bear his sorrow, he flew into the net too. The hunter came out of hiding and took the entire dove family home happily.

"Ignorant humans are no different from these birds. At times, they exult too much, and at other times have to face great pain. Bound by emotional attachment, they lose their reasoning power and meet their end along with family. Those who waste their noble human birth in this way can be compared to people who let loose their hold after reaching the tree top. I learnt from the doves that too much attachment with anyone or anything is not desirable.'

Here ends the seventh chapter. In the eighth chapter, the Lord describes what Maharṣi Dattātreya told Nimi about the next nine gurus he had learnt lessons from.

11.8.1-4: "Hé King! Human beings experience joy and sorrow. Both these are there in heaven and hell also. Therefore, know that there is no escape from such feelings. Do not try to satisfy the sense organs; this is an endless process. Pythons lie unmoved in a place and swallow whatever they get. Likewise, the wise eat whatever they get and go hungry at other times. Thus I learnt from the python that a true yogi does not care about his body or sense organs.

11.8.5-6: "The ocean is vast and deep. Its waters are clear. Nobody can dive freely to the bottom of the ocean to see what all are there. None can see its shore on the other side. A sage's intellect must be like that, deep, clear and unfathomable. Moreover, during the rainy season, rivers are full and they carry large quantities of water into the ocean. In summer, the amount of water that flows into the ocean is much less. Yet the ocean always looks the same. Similarly, an intelligent person is not affected by either prosperity or adversity.

11.8.7-8: "Moths are attracted to fire and they perish in it. Ignorant men are similarly attracted by women, wealth, clothes, jewellery etc., which ultimately destroy them. They spend a lifetime chasing these, and finally die. Thus I learnt from moths that desire leads to ruin.

11.8.9-10: "A sage must consume only that much food that is essential to maintain his body. To get this much food, he should not trouble one householder; he should visit more than one house and collect only small quantities of alms from each house. The sage must be like beetles which visit many flowers to collect food. This is what I learnt from beetles. Moreover, beetles take only nectar from flowers, whether big or small. Similarly, the wise must absorb only the essence of different scriptures.

11.8.11-12: "A sanyāsi should not store the alms that he collects for the evening or the next day. His hands should be the vessel for receiving the alms and his stomach the place to keep them. He should not be like bees who store the nectar they collect. The bees get killed when their hives are pressed for honey. Similarly, sanyāsis who store alms will also be ruined.

11.8.13-14: "A sage should not touch even a wooden statue of a woman, even with his legs. If he does, he will fall a prey to lust, just like male (bull) elephants who long for physical intimacy with female (cow) elephants. If another stronger bull wishes to have her, he may enter into a fight with the first bull and may even kill him. Wise men should not be lustful.

11.8.15-16: "Misers do not give even part of their wealth to others. However, all their wealth is later enjoyed by others. This is like bees that collect nectar and store it, which is taken away later by honey collectors. In the same way, food from houses run by householders immersed in worldly pleasures is first consumed by Sanyāsis.

11.8.17-18: "Sanyāsis roaming in the forest should not listen to passionate songs. Deer, which are attracted by melodious songs sung by the hunter, run towards them and get trapped. This is what I learnt from deer. Maharṣi Ṛśyaśṛnga had developed interest in women on listening to their rustic songs and watching them dance. As a result, he had become their plaything.

11.8.19-21: "The taste of food is identified by the tongue. One who craves for tasty food to satisfy the tongue faces disaster like how fish that bite the bait are caught by fishermen. Moreover, it is easier to conquer other sense organs, in comparison to the tongue. Therefore, once the tongue is conquered, it will not be difficult to keep other sense organs under control.

11.8.22-29: "Long back, in the country of Videha, there was a prostitute by name Pingala. Hear what I learnt from her. Dressed up bewitchingly, she stood one day at the entrance of her house, with the intention of attracting some handsome and rich man. Every now and then, someone would appear, and she would hope that he might be interested in her. However, he would move on. As time clicked on, many men came and went. At times, she would go back inside the house; presently would come out again with renewed hope. In this way, it became midnight. Pingala's face fell. Greed for money and inability to earn it made her sad. Gradually, she developed a feeling of dispassion. From that, happy thoughts began to flood her mind. Dispassion is the sword that cuts one's binding to desires. Hé honourable king! One who is passionate does not want to cut off connection with his body. This is just like how an ignorant man does not shed his ego. Listen to the song she sang, when her mind became free of all desires."

The next thirteen verses are sung by Pingala, as told by Maharṣi

Dattātreya to Emperor Nimi.

11.8.30-42: 'Pingala sang, "Just see the depth of my desires! Not having been able to conquer my mind, I have been foolishly lusting for men. Giving up my real lord, who is within me and never leaves me, and who gives everlasting happiness to me, I, being ignorant, have been seeking refuge in someone who can never give me happiness, who only increases my sadness, fear and never ending desires. My mind had to suffer sorrow because I took to a most deplorable profession. Lustfully, I craved for money and pleasure from disgraceful men unknown to me. What a fool I have been! Which intelligent person would give any value to this human body made of limbs and bones and the like, and covered by skin and hair? Forgetting the eternal God existing in this body, I have been running after reprehensible men. I am the only unwise person in this city of knowledgeable people.

"God is one's friend and protector and is the seat of ultimate bliss. I shall surrender this body to Him, and be with Him, just like how Goddess Lakṣmi remains with Viṣṇu. Men and gods who can provide sensual pleasures are subject to birth and death and are scared of Time; as such, how can any of them give everlasting joy to a wife? I am indeed fortunate because Lord Viṣṇu has been pleased with me, even though I have lived a life of shame till now. This is because by His grace, I have become totally detached from this materialistic world now. When one is attached to family and friends, one will not have peace of mind. As long as one's mind is not at peace, liberation is not possible. And for peace of mind, dispassion is most essential. In short, I am sure that this dispassion that I am experiencing now is because God has been kind to me. I accept this feeling that God has gracefully bestowed on me respectfully. I shall discard all desires and take refuge in Him. I shall remain contented with whatever I get. Knowing that the ultimate bliss can be provided only by Him, I shall take Him to be my husband and live with Him happily. With this firm resolve, I am surrendering myself to Him. He is the only one who can rescue me, groping my way with eyes blinded by desires, and bitten by the snake of Time, from this well, which is the world. One realises that the whole universe is controlled by Time when he or she develops total dispassion. And it is then that the Supreme Being manifests as the real protector."

Maharṣi Dattātreya continued:

11.8.43-44: "Thus, Pingala, on discarding the unholy craving for men, achieved mental harmony and went to bed peacefully. From her I learnt that desire causes grief and its absence leads to joy.'

In the next chapter, Lord Kṛṣna completes telling Uddhava the story of Maharṣi Dattātreya and Emperor Nimi.

In the first two ślokās of this chapter, the Maharṣi tells the emperor what he learnt from the hawk-like bird Osprey.

11.9.1-2: "One who understands that accepting possessions will ultimately lead to sorrow does not run after them. Such a person finds happiness. I saw that when an osprey with a piece of meat in its beak was attacked fiercely by some stronger birds, he gave it up and flew away in peace.

11.9.3-4: "Little children are not concerned about praise or insult. They have no worries like elders who have their family and homes. They keep on playing happily on their own. Like these children, we must experience joy within. Thus only two types of people live happy lives – little children who are not bothered about anything and the enlightened who have attained God.

11.9.5-10: 'Once, there was a girl of marriageable age, living with her parents. One day, in the absence of the parents, some relations went to her house with a marriage proposal. The girl welcomed them and gave them proper seats. She had to give them food, but there was no rice in the house at that time. So she began pounding paddy in a mortar. Then the bangles on her wrists made tingling sounds. She did not wish the guests to know what she was doing, and so, she removed all but two bangles from each wrist. Some sound could still be heard. So she took out one more bangle from each wrist and continued with pounding the paddy.

From this girl, I learnt that if many people live together, there will be noises and arguments. If two live together, then also there will be conversations. So a sage should live and move about alone. Only then will he get peace of mind for introspection and contemplation.

11.9.11-13: "One should, by practice, be able to control one's mind. By concentrating on the work at hand, one will be able to forget everything else. This method is useful to sages who want to practice dispassion, and annihilate Rajoguṇa and Tamoguṇa by Satvaguṇa. Once, with utmost concentration, a blacksmith was making arrows. At that time, his king went that way in a colourful procession. The entire neighbourhood ran to watch the grand procession. Yet the blacksmith did not see it or even hear the commotion! From the blacksmith, I learnt the worth of concentration.

11.9.14-15: "A sage should be a man of few words, travelling alone, with no permanent residing place. Getting a house built for this mortal body will lead to bindings one after another. Therefore, like a snake that lives in burrows made by others, a sage should desist from making his own house.

11.9.16-21: "Those who have freed themselves from all worldly bondages can realize God. The entire universe is born out of God. He stirs His own Māya consisting of the three Guṇās with Time, which is again His own form, to create the Universe. When the time comes, it dissolves in God too. For the creation of the universe, He does not need anything. This can be explained by the example of a spider. The spider produces a silk-like thread from its mouth and weaves a web with it. After some time, it withdraws the web into itself.

11.9.22-23: "The Jīvātma gets that form on which it fixes its mind. For example, larvae of insects like the mud wasp metamorphose into adult insects over time.

11.9.24: "In this way, I learnt many lessons from different teachers. In addition to all these, my own body is a guru too. Listen to what I learnt from my body.

11.9.25-27: "This body of mine, which is mortal, is also my

teacher, for it helps me to practise dispassion and refinement. It is well known that the body is born, goes through many experiences and finally dies. I am therefore not attached to it and I roam around freely. People earn wealth to fulfil their desires. They beget wives and children and other relatives, own money, animals and houses and get the service of servants. However, the human body, like a plant, comes to an end after giving rise to the next generation. Jñānendriyās and Karmendriyās, and hunger, thirst and the like, pull the body in different directions. This is similar to how the many wives of a householder approach him with diverse needs.

11.9.28-29: "Creating various types of plants, animals, snakes, fish, birds, insects etc. did not give enough satisfaction to the Creator. Only when he created human beings, did he get full gratification because only the human body, attained after experiencing the life of multitudes of other creatures, is capable of working towards obtaining mokṣa. Enjoyment of material pleasures is possible in all bodies, but only human beings have the wisdom to realize that everything is mortal.'

11.9.30-31: "It was because of such analysis of facts that I developed dispassion towards everything mortal. Acquiring this knowledge has helped me to live without ego and travel freely unattached to anyone or anything. Knowledge gained from one teacher will not be complete unlike that from many teachers. Great Ṛṣis proclaim in diverse ways that 'Brahmam' is one and never more than one."

Thus Sage Dattātreya spoke about his twenty four gurus from whom he had learnt invaluable lessons in life. Lastly, he said that his own body was also a guru for him. In the end, he indicated that everything in this vast universe can be considered as a guru, because God is one and omnipresent.

Śrī Kṛṣṇa continued:

11.9.32-33: "Emperor Yadu was satisfied with the explanations given by the supremely gifted Maharṣi and prostrated before him. Pleased that the emperor understood his advice fully, Sage Dattātreya went away a contented man. I am quite happy that the emperor, our ancestor, lived the rest of his life as per the advice of the wise sage, his mind fixed on the Supreme Being."

Here ends the ninth chapter of the eleventh canto. The next chapter begins with Lord Kṛṣṇa continuing his advice to Uddhava.

11.10.1: "Follow these directions. Lead a virtuous life free of desires, taking refuge in me.

11.10.2-7: "One whose intelligence is clear should ponder why people with worldly cravings get desired results only at times and not always. Those who are asleep see many things in their dreams, and those who are in an imaginary world also dream of many things. Just like these objects are not real, the physical body is also not real.

"Karmās should not be done desirous of results. Those who wish to know the ultimate truth should do only such karmās that will help them to be released from the cycle of birth and death. They should follow the rules prescribed in the scriptures and listen to their precepts who are stable-minded and represent me. They should be free from ego, unhealthy competitions and jealousy. They must be kind, intelligent, patient and inquisitive and should not indulge in false speech. They must show equanimity in associations with their spouses, children, other relations, and all forms of wealth as none of this is permanent.

11.10.8-34: "Though there exists fire in firewood, it will manifest only on burning the firewood, when it gives out light and heat. Firewood and fire are different, though they exist together. Similarly, though the soul exists in the body, its presence can be known only by contemplation. Fire can be small or big; it has a beginning and an end. These qualities of fire are based on the size of the firewood. The fact is that fire is there in an invisible form in all inflammable articles. In the same way, the soul appears to have qualities, though it is one and immortal.

"The body, formed of the pancabhūtās is mortal. A true seeker of knowledge must therefore realize the difference between the body and the soul, which will help him in shedding his ego. This will become easier if he approaches a noble guru and gets valuable instruction from him. True knowledge destroys the sense of plurality in the world. It is the jīvās that experience the results of various karmās done by individuals. So they are not freed from joys and sorrows and go through innumerable cycles of births and deaths.

"Joys and sorrows are experienced by both the intelligent and the ignorant. In such a situation, it is meaningless for the intelligent to feel proud. Even those who know how to beget joys and shun sorrows do not know how to avoid death and are in constant fear of death. As death is a reality and no one knows exactly when that will happen, everyone lives in fear of death. Just like on this earth, competition, envy, decline and destruction exist in swarga (heaven) as well. Therefore, accomplishment of heaven is not the final goal either. Suppose one lives righteously and attains swarga. There, he enjoys the fruits of his good deeds on earth and lives a carefree life surrounded by beautiful celestial maidens, listening to the melodious songs sung by gandharvās, playing in heavenly gardens of Devās and travelling around in aeroplanes controlled by mind power. Living thus in ultimate luxury, he does not know that the fruits of his good deeds are gradually waning and he will fall down from heaven in due time, despite his earnest prayers.

"Those who keep bad company and are immersed in desires throughout their lives and perform evil deeds, those who kill animals without rhyme or reason and worship spirits go to hell and are later born in lowly wombs or as plants or such immovable living beings. What joy do such people get from living as various creatures over and over again? Thus the worlds which exist till the deluge and their protectors, in fact everyone, is scared of me; even the Creator whose life span is enormously long, is no exception to this.

"Indriyās give rise to karmās because gunās motivate them. Finally, Jīvās, proud of the indriyās, experience the consequences of the karmās. Ātma is above and beyond all this. As long as one is ignorant of this truth, his fear will remain. The actual truth is that I am the whole universe and all its features like Kālam (Time), Ātma (Soul) Dharmam (Righteousness) and the like."

Listening to this discourse, Uddhava had some doubts:

11.10.35-37: "Detachment is necessary as attachments exist; how do attachments form and how can they be destroyed? How can those people who have released themselves from bondage be distinguished from others? How can the soul be both in bondage and free at the same time?"

The answers to these questions given by the Lord are seen in the next chapter.

11.11.1-25: "The feeling of attachment is because of Guṇās, which is caused by my māya. Thus, I have no attachment and no detachment. Occurrence of joy and sorrow, birth and death of bodies, are all unreal. Understand that everything in this world is illusory. All that we come to know with the help of our sense organs and all that we think about and imagine to be real are not real. Ignorance leads to bondage or bandha and knowledge leads to liberation or Mokṣa. Both ignorance and knowledge are two forms of my māya. If one realises this truth, there is no question of attachment. How can one feel attached to things that are non-existent?

"Secondly, bondage and freedom do not exist together at the same time in the same place. It is a myth that Paramātma is free and Jīvātma is in bondage. However, in one's ignorant state, it is so. As long as one is ignorant, he thinks that the bonded Jīvātma and the free Paramātma coexist in his body. When one becomes enlightened, this illusory bondage disappears. I shall tell you now, dear disciple, the differences between the bonded and the liberated. The former face the consequences of their karmās as they take their bodies to be true. The latter know that the real self is not the body and behave accordingly. Therefore, those who have attained true knowledge are never arrogant. The jīvās in the bodies of the ignorant think that it is they who perform the karmās. Such people take pride in their actions. The wise know that they have no ownership in anything they do, just like the sun, sky or air. Because of this dispassion, they are never bonded. Their intellect is sharper due to this dispassion; their concepts are clear and so they disregard the plurality in the universe. So even when they live in their physical bodies, they are not controlled by sense organs. In that sense, they are the truly liberated. They will not be bothered by external experiences as their minds are steadfast. They will not be angry with those who insult them or flattered by those who praise them either. True sages do not do anything wrong and do not say anything wrong. They will not have any wrong thoughts either. Immersed in perpetual bliss, they wander about aimlessly like innocent children. The energies of those who are well-versed in scriptures and yet are not able to actualize the Paramātma are like the efforts put in by those who look after cows that do not yield milk.

"Hé Uddhava, those who put up with unfaithful wives and wicked sons, who hoard superfluous money without giving it away to the needy, who do not glorify me, and who are attached to their mortal bodies experience sorrow after sorrow. On the other hand, those who speak about my deeds, and know me to be the origin, maintenance, and dissolution of the universe purify themselves and others. The assumption that there are many souls is wrong. Get rid of this assumption. Shun the desire to perform karmās – this desire is caused by rajoguṇa. Fix your mind free of rajoguṇa in the omnipresent me. Have total faith in me. If it is not possible to evade performing karmās, do them without thinking of their fruit. If you succeed in this, you will automatically become a true devotee and will be interested in listening to my stories which purify the whole world. Then you will depend only on me and none else. The best method to develop such unflinching devoutness is association with the noble. They will show you the right path, travelling along which the devotee reaches his destination rapidly."

At this juncture, Uddhava asked Kṛṣṇa a few questions.

11.11.26-28: "Hé Lord of the Universe! What are the signs of good people and true devotees who are dear to you? I love and respect you immensely, and have taken refuge in you. You are the Supreme Being; it is only that you have incarnated on the Earth in this particular form. Please be kind enough to clear all my doubts."

The Lord replied:

11.11.29-33: "A noble person dear to me possesses many qualities. He will not hurt others. He will instead be kind, tolerant, truthful, helpful, pure of heart, calm, and stable-minded. He will have controlled his desires and ego, have an analytical mind, be intelligent, will have taken refuge in me and will eat moderately. He will be patient and courageous, respect others, be friendly with everyone, magnanimous, and far-sighted. He will have conquered hunger, thirst, sorrow, desires, old age, and death. He will not expect recognition from others. He who worships me, leaving aside everything else, is the noblest person. He may or may not know my form; yet he adores me."

After describing the signs of devotees in this way, Lord Kṛṣṇa went on to explain all about devotion.

11.11.34-40: "True devotees can be identified by many signs. Seeing, touching, worshipping, glorifying, respecting, and serving my idols and devotees; listening attentively my stories, meditating on my form, offering everything to me, surrendering everything, including oneself, to me in service, praising my birth and deeds, celebrating my birthday, conducting festivals of vocal and instrumental music, dance, concerts etc. in my temples; taking my idol around generating devotion in the onlookers, undertaking periodic fasting as per prescribed rites, taking interest individually and collectively in constructing temples, parks, gardens, inns etc., keeping own houses and temples spotlessly clean, being selfless and pure, not being proud or boastful, not having a feeling of ownership in the various items offered to me, are all marks of my devotees.

11.11.41-47: "Offer me things in the world that you like best. By doing so, you will get infinite blessings. The main seats where I can be worshipped are the sun, fire, Brāhmins, cows, devotees of Mahāviṣnu, space, air, water, earth, soul in the body, and all Bhūtās. Worship sun with Vedās, fire with havan objects, Brāhmins with hospitality, cows with grass and water etc., devotees of Viṣnu with cordial and warm conduct, space in the heart with meditation, air with the realization that it is Prāṇa itself, water with flowers and the like mixed with water, earth with mantras written on it, soul in the body with good practices, and me present in the Bhūtās with equanimity in all that is created. In all these places, worship my serene form singlemindedly with conch, discus, mace and lotus in my four arms. One who worships me in this way with absolute concentration will soon become my ardent devotee and realize me.

11.11.48-49: "Hé Uddhava, there is no better method to obtain me other than association with the devoted. Hé noblest among Yādavās, as you are pure hearted and are my beloved friend, I shall now reveal to you some secrets"

Here ends the eleventh chapter of the eleventh canto. The Lord continues his discourse in the next chapter.

11.12.1-15: "Practices like yoga, philosophical analysis, studying the vedās, and performing karmās as given in them desire less of good results, charity, penance, yāgās, mantrās etc. do not appeal to me, as much as association with devotees or satsang. Hé sinless Uddhava, as a result of satsang, even lesser evolved creatures like birds, bears, monkeys, elephants, asurās with excess of rājasik or tāmasik gunās, and the like have attained mokṣa in different yugās. Some examples are Vṛtrāsura, Prahlāda, Sugrīva, Hanumān, Jatāyu, Gajendra, Bāṇāsura, Mahābali, Maya, Vibhīṣaṇa, Jāmbavān etc. Likewise, Kubja, Gopa maidens, devotee wives of the Brahmaṇās etc. never learnt the vedās or served great men, or performed penances. Some snakes (like Kāliya), trees (like those in Vṛndāvan) etc., despite being born with low intelligence, were also liberated. Gopikās were so much in love with me that they felt the long time I spent with them was very short, just a few seconds. They could not bear the thought of separation from me when I was going to Mathura. They felt the time I spent in Mathura was equivalent to ages. On account of absolute surrender to me, they attained Brahman, that is, me. They are devotees of the highest level, higher than ṛṣis and maharṣis. Therefore, Uddhava, you may forget the vedās and śāstrās. Just know that I am all in all; be fearless and take refuge in me."

Even after hearing all this, Uddhava was not fully free of doubts. He told Śrī Kṛṣṇa:

11.12.16: "Lord of all gods! Even after listening to your words so far, some of my reservations remain. I am confused."

The Lord replied:

11.12.17-24: "The Lord of the Universe manifests as the Universe by His power of illusion. He is the subtle as well as the gross. Heat and light are latent in fire, and fire is there in a piece of wood also. That is why when two pieces of wood are rubbed against each other, sparks are formed which with the help of air burst into a flame, emanating heat and light. Here, subtle is being converted into gross. Similarly, words made of letters are the outward manifestation of me. Just like sound, all other senses also are expressions of mine. Same is the case with mind, intellect, ego etc. The one and only God has always been there; and the entire creation has originated from Him. If the universe is a cloth, God is the thread that forms the cloth. The tiny embryo in a seed grows into a huge tree with a trunk, many branches, roots, leaves, flowers and fruits. The former therefore represents the tree in a miniscule form. Similarly, the various living beings and non-living things in the universe are derived from the original entity that is God. One who understands this truth releases himself from ignorance and gets unified with the Supreme."

The first seven verses of the next chapter are also spoken by Lord Kṛṣṇa.

11.13.1-7: "The three gunās are characteristic of the intellect and not the soul. When only sātvik food and drinks are used and only righteous thoughts are nurtured in the mind, devotion will sprout automatically in the mind and it will grow day by day. This devotion, which is an offshoot of satvaguṇa, will extinguish rajoguṇa and tamoguṇa completely. Finally, as satvaguṇa gets refined more and more, it disappears by itself. Performing virtuous deeds, behaving in a cultured manner, chanting the names of God, meditation and the like enhance satvaguṇa. Condemning these make one tāmasik. Being indifferent to sātvik qualities makes one rājasik. Sātvik people will gain true knowledge, and their sense of ego will disappear. A fire that originates by friction between bamboo shoots consumes the entire bamboo jungle. In the same way, when devotion and knowledge touch the highest peak, the jīvan does not accumulate any pāpa or puṇya as neither good nor bad karmās are performed. It is liberated from the cycle of births and deaths."

At this juncture, Uddhava wanted to get another doubt cleared. He asked the Lord:

11.13.8: "Hé Kṛṣṇa! Most people know that desires are the root cause of sorrows; yet they do not give up desires, just like animals such as dogs, donkeys, goats etc. that go after whatever they want, even while facing danger. Why so?"

The answer to this query is given by Kṛṣṇa in six verses.

11.13.9-14: "The ignorant think that the body is everything. In their minds, rajoguṇa dominates satvaguṇa. They therefore are victims of intense desire. They make plans to implement specific jobs. Despite knowing that the ultimate result will be only grief, they keep on performing various karmās, unable to conquer their senses. The wise, on the other hand, even if influenced by rājasik and tāmasik intelligence, try again and again, without hesitation, to unify the mind with ātma. With time, they leave behind all desires. Therefore, they do not get demoralised. Try to control breath consciously as much as possible, and leave everything to me. This is yoga. This was the advice I gave to the Maharṣis Sanaka and his brothers."

Uddhava then wanted to know this entire incident. He said:

11.13.15: "Hé Keśava! I would like to know when, and in which form, you gave such invaluable advice to Sanaka and others."

Kṛṣṇa replied:

11.13.16-21: "Once, the four rishi brothers Sanaka, Sananda, Sanātana and Sanalkumāra asked the same question that you have put to me, to Brahma, their father. They wanted to know how a person who was desirous of salvation would withdraw his mind from desires. The creator, despite being immersed in meditation for long periods, did not know the precise answer as his intellect was always busy with the process of creation. So he pondered over the question for long. Finally, he thought of me. Then I took the form of a haṁsaṁ (swan) and went and sat near them. A swan, as you know, can separate milk from water. I wanted to show them that I could explain the truth, seeking it out of all untruths, and so I took the form of a swan. Seeing me, Sanaka and his brothers asked me who I was. Hé Uddhava! Listen now to the answer I gave them to this and other questions of theirs."

The next nineteen verses, from 11.13.22 to 11.13.40 together are famed as the Haṁsagīta. The Lord concludes his rendition in the next two verses, forty one and forty two. This whole part of Uddhavagīta is given in detail in Chapter 11.

The first and second verses of the next chapter are spoken by Uddhava. He is continuing his doubt clearing session with the Lord.

11.14.1-2: "Hé Kṛṣṇa! Authorities on Vedās state that there are various methods to attain deliverance. Tell me, Kṛṣṇa, are all of them equally effective or some better than others? To reach the highest level, one should be a true devotee. How does one become a true devotee?"

Lord Kṛṣṇa answered these two questions in great detail.

11.14.3-30: "As for your first question, yes, there are different views on the best method to follow for liberation. This is so because the Vedās were destroyed in the great deluge, and at the beginning of creation that followed, I had explained to the creator that the highest dharma is to fix one's mind on me. Brahma imparted this knowledge to his son Manu, from whom the seven chief Maharṣis, famed as the Saptarṣis, received it. From them, their numerous sons like the Devās, Asurās, Gandharvās, Sidhās, Vidyādharās, Kinnarās, Nagās, humans and many others obtained this knowledge. However, based on their respective Guṇās, they understood the truth differently. Their intellects were of different types and levels. As a result of this, the interpretations came to be different. Each one firmly believed that his interpretation was the best. They argued differently that the highest value should be given to truth, charity, prosperity, desires, yagyās, fame, truth, controlling mind, conquering senses, penance, rituals, rules and regulations etc. etc. Accordingly, their actions varied too. Actually, all these provide only temporary happiness. How can supporters of these theories achieve the everlasting bliss available to those who are disinterested in anything but me? Those who have conquered their indriyās and controlled their mind experience absolute joy. They do not wish for the position of Indra in heaven or that of the king of the netherworld; nor do they crave for mastery over miracles or even freedom from birth and death. They only wish for union with me.

My devotees are very dear to me. For example, my love towards you is more than my love to my son Brahma or my grandson Śiva or my elder brother Balarāma or my wife Lakṣmi. I accompany my devotees wherever they go, for I believe that the dust from their feet purify everything. Others can never fathom the depth of my affection to my devotees. Just like fire burns fuel wood fully, undiluted devotion in me eradicates all sins of devotees. Yoga, knowledge, morality, proficiency in vedās, charity – nothing attracts me more than devotion. Even the most horrible sins can be absolved by developing devotion to me. Truth, compassion, knowledge, penance etc. do not purify one's mind if these are not accompanied by piety. When one has unqualified devotion, he becomes soft hearted and sheds tears of joy. True devotees cry and laugh, and sing and dance without ignominy when they feel unified with me. Their hearts melt and their words tremble and they purify the whole world. Like how dirt is removed from gold on heating, when impurities are burnt out because of bhakti, mind is cleansed. Those who listen to my tales and tell others the same gradually start seeing me, like how those with diseased eyes begin seeing perfectly well on application of the right medicine. The mind of one who is immersed in worldly thoughts get fixed on worldly objects, but that of one who remembers me at all times dissolves in me. Therefore, stop thinking of illusory objects and fix your mind, purified by meditation, in me. When one loses interest in women, he loses interest in the whole world. So do not get in the company of women who distract your attention.

Instead, sit in an isolated place and meditate on me."

At this, Uddhava wished to know how to proceed on the path of meditation.

11.14.31: "Hé lotus-eyed! Which form of yours should I meditate on? Kindly elaborate to me everything about dhyāna yoga."

Śrī Bhagvān began:

11.14.32-46: "Sit straight in a comfortable pose, place your hands on your lap and look at the tip of your nose. Do Pūrakam by taking air inside through inhalation, then do Kumbhakam by retaining air inside the lungs and then do Recakam by releasing air outward through exhalation. Repeat the process. This clears the respiratory tracts. Doing these three in the reverse order also has the same effect. While doing these, control your senses and mind and concentrate only on the breath. Gradually, over days of practice, the whole process will become easier. Later, while doing this Prāṇāyāmam, become aware of the 'Aūṁ' sound always present in the heart and fix it there. 'Aūṁ' is the Praṇava mantra. While practising this technique, the mind will not waver anywhere. Do it thrice a day – before dawn, at mid-day and at dusk, ten times each. In one month, you can win over your own Prāṇā. Look inwards and see that the heart is shaped like an inverted lotus bud. Now, gradually, imagine it as an open flower, with eight petals, facing upwards. See sun, moon and fire, one above the other, in the centre of this flower. In the centre of the fire globe at the top, see me, perfectly formed, peaceful, beautiful, with four long arms, long, attractive neck, glowing cheeks and a charming smile, with ornaments on symmetrical ears, wearing a silk robe of golden hue, blackish in complexion like a rain cloud, the Śrīvatsa scar and Śrīdevi on the left and right sides of my chest, with conch, discus, mace and lotus on my hands and floral garland on my chest, wearing the lustrous Kaustubha gem on my neck, feet decorated with anklets, shining crown, bangles, waist band, clear and pretty eyes on a pleasant face – in short, beautiful all over. Meditate on this lovely form, first part by part and then fully, all the while keeping your senses away and without letting the intellect pulling the mind away from me. Without thinking of anything else, meditate on my whole form first and then fix your attention fully on my smiling face. Further, draw your mind from that and concentrate on the sky. Then, taking refuge in me, do not think of anything. In this way, one who has his mind fixed on me, the universal soul has become one with me, like a spark uniting with a flame. Thus, through this powerful method of meditation, a yogi sheds all illusions and easily attains mokṣa."

The first śloka of the next chapter is also spoken by the Lord.

11.15.1: "A yogi who has conquered his indriyās and controlled his breathing, and without getting distracted, has his mind fixed on me attains various siddhīs."

At this, Uddhava asked Kṛṣṇa:

11.15.2: "Hé Immortal one! You are the giver of siddhīs. So please tell me how many types of siddhīs there are and how they can be accomplished."

The rest of the chapter, from verses three to thirty eight, comprise the Lord's answer to these questions. He said:

11.15.3-8: "There are mainly eighteen types of siddhīs. Of these, eight are more important as they help in attaining me. With the siddhi named 'Aṇima', one can make his body very tiny; with 'Mahima', enormously huge and with 'Laghima', exceptionally light in weight. 'Prākāśyam' is the siddhi with which one can know about everything in this world and the other. 'Prāpti' helps one to be able to enjoy all the pleasures that can be experienced with the help of the sense organs of all living beings. Using the siddhi 'Īśitva', one can make others do whatever one wants him to. With 'Vaśitva', one can remain mentally aloof from his body and sense organs. 'Kāmāvasāyita' or 'Prākāmya' assists one to achieve instantly whatever one wishes for. These eight siddhīs ever exist in me. (In some other texts, 'Garima', the ability to make one's body extremely heavy, is one of the eight Sidhīs. In this system, 'Prākāśyam' is not seen.)

In addition to these, there are fifteen more siddhīs, which are secondary in nature. The first set of ten secondary siddhis are anūrmimatvam – not being troubled by hunger, thirst, sorrow, desire, wrinkles in old age, and death; dūraśravaṇam and dūradarśanam – ability to hear and see, respectively, living and non-living things far away; manojavam – ability to reach places instantly where thought goes; kāmarūpam – ability to assume any desired form; parakāyapraveśanam – ability to make one's jīvan enter into another's body; svacchandamṛtyu – to be able to die when one wishes to; devānām krīdānudarśanam – capability to see and enjoy the pastimes of gods and goddesses; yatha sankalpasamsiddhi – accomplishing the end results as dreamt; and ājñāpratihatā gatiḥ – ability to reach any place without any obstruction.

The second set of five such siddhīs are trikālajñatvam – knowing the past, present and future; advandvam – tolerance of heat, cold and other dualities; paracitta ādi abhijñatā – knowing the minds etc. of others; agni arka ambu viṣa ādīnām pratiṣṭambhanam – the ability to overcome the influence of fire, sun, water, poison etc. and aparājayah – remaining unconquered by anyone."

After enumerating the siddhīs, the Lord proceeds to explain how to attain these by firm determination. He said:

11.15.9-32: "I have told you briefly all about the various siddhīs. Now hear from me how these can be attained by various resolutions. Everything is present in its subtle form in me. So, by meditating on me, one can achieve anima. By expanding the mind or by meditating separately on any bhūta like the sky, one can get mahima. When one is able to concentrate on the minutest particles or atoms in me, he gets laghima. By meditating on the active principles in me, one gets the sidhi of prākāśyam.

"By concentrating on the sātvik aspect of me, one gets prāpti. Focussing on all the three Guṇās as my attributes helps one to achieve īśitva. Fixing one's mind on me, Nārāyaṇa, in the fourth state of turīyam, makes one eligible for the siddhi vaśitva. Whoever meditates with a pure heart on me, complete in all respects, devoid of any guṇa, achieves desireless absolute bliss – and this is kāmāvasāyita' or 'prākāmya'. [Contemplating on my gross form begets garima.]

"By envisioning on me, fair in complexion and righteousness personified, one gets the siddhi of anūrmimatvam. One who can listen to the sound present in me, the prāṇa of all, achieves dūraśravaṇam. When one is able to see the sun in his eye and his eye in the sun, thereby unifying both, and meditates on me in this combined form, he gets the siddhi of dūradarśanam. By joining his mind, body and prāṇa with me, a person will get the capability to travel to any place which he thinks of. This is manojavam. One who takes unqualified refuge in my yogic power can take whatever form he wishes to – this is the siddhi of kāmarūpam.

"A yogi who wishes to enter another's body should meditate on his jīvan in the other's body; then, his Prāṇa will leave his body, making him lifeless temporarily. Then, as air, the siddha can enter the other's lifeless body through his nose, making him alive. This is parakāyapraveśanam. (Whenever he wishes, he can return to his original body.)

"A yogi who wishes to have svacchandamṛtyu can achieve that by a certain procedure. He should close his anal orifice with his heel and lift his prāṇa successively to his heart, chest, neck, head, and finally let it go out through brahmarandhra (the fine pore on the top of his head, in the centre) as soon as he becomes one with brahma. His life force will thus leave his body.

"Those yogis who wish to roam around in the garden of the gods and goddesses should meditate on the satvaguṇa in me. Goddesses who have their origin in satvaguṇa will appear before them in celestial aeroplanes and take them to their garden. This siddhi is called devānām krīdānudarśanam.

"A yogi who contemplates on me as truth itself and firmly believes that I am the realizer of all dreams, achieves yatha sankalpa-samsiddhi or sankalpasiddhi. Whatever he imagines comes true.

"I am the one who commands and am unconditionally free. A yogi who has become like me in this respect has achieved the siddhi ājña or ājñāpratihatā gatiḥ, i.e. his command is obeyed by all and he can go wherever he wants without any obstacle.

"A yogi who has undiluted bhakti in me and knows my

attributes becomes a trikālajñāni. He knows all about the past, present and future of everyone and everything.

"One who meditates on me, indifferent about the Guṇās seen in nature, gets the siddhi of advandvam. He will not complain about heat or cold or any other pairs of opposites.

"By contemplating on me present in the hearts of all, witnessing everything, yogis achieve paracittajñānam. They can read the minds of all. A yogi whose mind is merged with my attributes accomplishes agni-ādīnām pratiṣṭambhanam. His yogic body will not burn, without his consent, if fire engulfs him, neither will his body drown in water. All the bhūtās will cooperate with him, like how animals living in water take to water naturally. One who meditates on the forms of my incarnations with weapons etc. can never be defeated by anyone – they have got the siddhi aparājayam."

Lord Kṛṣṇa then concludes his discourse on this topic thus:

11.15.33-38: "Yogis who meditate on all aspects of mine possess all these siddhīs. They have conquered their indriyās, withdrawn from all externalities, and controlled their minds and prāṇās and are engrossed in thinking about me; which siddhi is not accessible to them? However, yogis who wish to be one with me should not work for or long for siddhīs, for they are obstacles in their path. I am the cause of all siddhīs. I am also the cause of dharma and mokṣa. I am the guardian of all and the giver of the result for everything. I am Īśwara; I advise brahmajñāna to those who deserve it. All beings are made of pancabhūtās. The bhūtās are also present outside all beings. Similarly, I exist within all and also outside all."

Here ends the fifteenth chapter.

In the initial five verses of the next chapter, the pious Uddhava sings the glory of Bhagvān Kṛṣṇa and requests the Lord to enlighten him about how great Maharṣīs acquire the ultimate siddhi.

11.16.1-5: "You are one with neither beginning nor end. You are pure Brahmam and birth, sustenance and destruction of all depend on you. You are present in all the Bhūtās, but even while seeing the Bhūtās, the ignorant do not see you as they are affected by Māya. Only the enlightened know the real significance of the Vedās and worship you appropriately. In what form do they worship you to get the most crucial siddhi? Also, kindly tell me where all your manifestations can be perceived in the three worlds – heaven, earth and netherworld. I prostrate before you, O Supreme Being."

Most of the succeeding ślokās of this chapter are devoted to Lord Kṛṣṇa's elaborate reply to this question.

11.16.6-8: "Hé noblest among those who ask questions! The question you have asked me now was put forward to me by Arjuna in the Kurukṣetra, when he was about to engage in the great war with his enemies. All of a sudden, he felt that fighting with relations was a heinous crime. At the thought that he would have to kill them in the war, he decided not to fight at all, and wished to turn back from Kurukṣetra. To the questions he asked me at that time, I gave appropriate answers. One of the questions was exactly the same as you are asking me now. So listen to what I told him then.

11.16.9-19: "Hé Uddhava! I am the soul, guardian and master of all the Bhūtās. I create, sustain and destroy them. I am the destination of those who strive to reach their goal. For those who win over everything, I am Time, for, time wins over all. I am the stability of Guṇās and am the Guṇa of each substance. Of the Sātviks, I am intelligence; of the smallest entities, I am Jīvan and among all that are most difficult to conquer, I am mind. I am Brahma among teachers of the Vedās. Among mantrās, I am 'aum', and among letters, a. In meters in the Vedās, I am the syllable.

"I am Indra among the Devās and Agni among the 'Vasus'. In the midst of the sons of Aditi and Kaśyapa, I am Vāmana, Viṣṇu's incarnation and among the various Rudrās, Nīlalohita. Among Brahmarṣis, I am Bhṛgu; among Rājarṣis, Manu; and among Devarṣis, Nārada. Among cows, I am Kāmadhenu, and among birds, Garuḍa. Among the great Siddhās, I am Kapila;

among Prajāpatis, Dakṣa; among the PitṛDevās, Aryamā; among Asurās, Prahlāda; and among Yakṣās, Kubera; and among the stars and the medicinal plants, their master the Moon.

"I am Airāvata among elephants; Varuna among inhabitants of water; Sūrya among the things that give light and heat; King among human beings; Uccaśravas among horses; gold among metals; Antaka among those who control others; Vāsuki among snakes; Ananta among serpents; Lion among animals with canines; Sanyāsa among the four āśramās; and the first among the varṇās. Pure hearted Uddhava, know all this.

11.16.20-28: "Amid running streams and rivers, I am Ganga; amid stationary water bodies, the ocean; amid mountains, Himālaya; amid trees, the banyan tree; amid weapons, the bow and amid archers, Paramaśiva. I am Yvam rice (barley) among medicines. Amidst teacher sages, I am Vasiṣṭha and amidst experts on Vedās, I am Bṛhaspati. Among army generals, I am Subrahmaṇya. I am the Brahmayāga among all yāgās, and ahimsa among vratās.

"I am air, fire, sun, water and words among things that purify other things. I am samādhi yoga among the eight limbs of yoga namely yamam, niyamam, āsanam, prānāyāmam, pratyāhāram, dhārana, dhyānam and samādhi. I am the thinking process of those who wish to succeed. Among judgements, I am ātmavidya which helps one to differentiate truth from untruth. Among those who debate for fame, I am the motion of the debate.

"Among women, I am Śatarūpa and among men, Brahma's son Manu; among sages, I am Nārāyaṇa and among brahmacāris, Sanatkumāra. Of all types of joys, I am the state of mind which does not wander here and there. In people of few words, I am good words and silence. In those who are always vigilant, I am the year, representing Time; Time is always alert. Among seasons, I am spring; among months, Mārgaśīrṣa (Dhanu); and among stars, Abhijit, the twenty-eighth and the brightest star. I am Kṛtam among yugās, Devala and Asita among the courageous, Vedavyāsa among those who classified Vedās, and Śukra among intelligent poets.

11.16.29-36: "I am Vāsudeva amidst gods, and amidst those who worship God, you. Amidst the able and brainy, I am Hanumān and among Vidyādharās, Sudarśana. I am Padmarāga among precious stones, lotus bud among beautiful things, Durva grass among grasses, and ghee from cow's milk among things used in havan.

"I am the riches of the hardworking, playing dice in cheats, endurance in the patient, and strength of the strong. Know that I am the physical forte and the mental power in the robust, and the actions of the devotees. I am Viśwavasu among the Gandharvās, and Pūrvacitti among Apsarās. I am the stability of mountains, fragrance of the earth, the essence of water, the brilliance in the sun, moon and stars and the supernatural sound in the sky, and the brightness in the fire.

"Among Brāhmin devotees, I am Bali, and among the heroic, I am Arjuna. I am the creator, preserver and destroyer of the Bhūtās. I am the master Indriya of all the ten Indriyās. Among the five karmendriyās, I am the power to speak in the vocal chords and tongue, the capacity to grasp things in hands, the ability to walk in the feet, the capability to excrete in the anus and the competence to procreate in the genitals. Similarly, I am the capability to hear, feel, see, taste and smell in the five jnānendriyās of ears, skin, eyes, tongue and nose respectively.

11.16.37-44: "I am the earth, water, light, ego and such other – in fact, the entire mahat-tattva consisting of twenty five tattvās, or the sum total of all material creation and true knowledge. Īśwara, Jīvan, Guṇās, Guṇīs etc. are seen in only me, the Paramātma, and nowhere else. It is possible to count and find out the number of sand particles on the earth if a sufficiently long time is available. However, it is not possible to count my characteristics; how I am continuously creating crores and crores of universes. Some of my features are eminence, prosperity, fame, prominence, shyness, sacrifice, beauty, fortune, heroism, patience, strength, knowledge etc. Wherever these qualities are seen, know that they indicate my presence.

"I am telling you all this for your benefit. However, these are all words, and words cannot describe my real nature. Control your words, mind, Prāṇās, and Indriyās with your intellect. Then, control your Rājasik intellect with your Sātvik intellect. After that, you will never have materialistic thoughts. If a sanyāsi is not able to keep his words and thoughts under control, his following rituals, penance and charitable acts will be useless like water stored in a raw earthen pot. When you conquer your mind, words and Prāṇa with your intellect devoted to me and taken refuge in me, your vicious cycle of births and deaths will come to an end."

The first seven Ślokās of the next chapter are spoken by Uddhava.

11.17.1-7: "From time immemorial, you have been determined to inculcate bhakti in people of all varnās and in all āśramās. Hé lotus-eyed! You are the only one who can enlighten me on what dhārmic deeds should be done so as to develop bhakti. Hé Supreme Being! The particulars of dharma that you, in the form of a divine swan, explained to Lord Brahma's sons in his presence, have been lost in the course of time. Hé immortal one! There is no one else who can give such advice even in an assemblage of the most enlightened in this world or any other. If you, the protector, leave this Earth, who will give such advice to the people here? Therefore, kindly tell me in detail all about the dharmās which help one to build unqualified devotion in you."

Maharṣi Śuka tells King Parīkṣit here:

11.17.8: "Lord Kṛṣṇa was very pleased to hear these words from the chief of his devotees. He then enumerated to Uddhava the various righteous deeds to be performed by all for their own benefit. Dharma is desirable at all times, in all places, and it benefits mankind immensely."

The rest of the chapter, from verses nine to fifty eight, is devoted to the Lord's discourse on the right deeds to be done by people of the four Varṇās (Brāhmanās, Kṣatriyās, Vaiśyās and Śūdrās), and the first two (Brahmacarya and Gārhasthya) of the four āśramās. The rest two (Vānaprastha and Sanyāsa) are discussed in the next chapter. The Lord said:

11.17.9-58: "Hé Uddhava! This question of yours will develop bhakti in people who follow the dharma of Varṇās and Āśramās. So listen to the answer from me. In the beginning, in the Kṛta Yuga, all were Sātvik and were of the same Varṇa, called Haṁsaṁ. They were born with all good qualities and remained so. At that time, Praṇavaṁ was the Vedaṁ and I was the Dharmaṁ. All worshipped me. As they were content, they had no desires, and so there was no need for any ritual.

"At the beginning of Tretā Yuga, the first three Vedās originated from me. As per the Vedās, yāgās came into practice. People of four Varṇās, i.e. Brāhmanās, Kṣatriyās, Vaiśyās and Śūdrās originated from the face, arms, thighs and feet of the Virāt Puruṣa, a manifestation of me, respectively. The Varṇa of each individual was based on his own conduct in life.

"The four āśramās also originated from me – Brahmacarya from heart, Gārhasthya from hip, Vānaprastha from chest, and Sanyāsa from head. The gradient of nobleness of the Varṇās and Āśramās thus came to be associated with their respective place of origin. However, it should not be forgotten that all parts of the body are necessary for its effective functioning.

The Brāhmanās have conquered their antaḥkaraṇa (mind, intellect, memory and ego) and controlled their Indriyās. They are clean, contented, tolerant, pure, kind, honest, philosophical, and devoted to me. The characteristics of Kṣatriyās are skill, physical and mental strength, fearlessness in war, capability to work hard and endure adverse times, kindness, stability, veneration to Brāhmanās, devotion to God etc. Trust in God, generosity, truthfulness, reverences to Brāhmanās, constant discontent in the wealth earned etc. are the traits of Vaiśyās. Taking refuge in Gods, serving Brāhmanās, being truthful, taking care of animals, being content with whatever is earned etc., make up the basic nature of Śūdrās.

"People of all the four Varṇās described till now have many good qualities and can intermingle with one another. However, there are people of a very inferior nature and they are grouped in a fifth Varṇa or Pancamavarṇa. Such people are unclean, dishonest, unfaithful, fighting with others unnecessarily, lustful, irate, and greedy – it is best to avoid them. People belonging to all Varṇās should be honest and kind to all creatures, and they should try to overcome lust, anger, greed etc.

"Now I shall tell you about what should be done in the different āśramṁs. In the Brahmacarya āśram, after the thread ceremony, a Brāhmin should approach a suitable precept and begin living in his hermitage as a disciple. He should learn to control his senses and learn the Vedās. He should be dressed in proper simple attire and develop locks in his hair. He should not shave. He should use simple vessels for drinking water and chant God's names using a Japamāla (rosary). His seat should be plain, unpainted, and undecorated. He should remain silent while taking bath, eating, performing havans etc.

"He should not shave off hair on any part of his body. A brahmacāri should not eject semen; if it does happen unknowingly, he should take a bath, do prāṇāyāmam and chant Gāyatri. He should worship the Sun, Fire, cows, teachers, elders, Devās etc., speak only when necessary, and pray with total concentration at dawn and dusk. Respect to the preceptor should be absolute, as he is the personification of the Gods. He should not insult his guru or be jealous of him.

"A brahmacāri should collect alms from households, and partake it only after feeding his preceptor well. He should be humble and serve his teacher at all times. In this way, with utmost discipline, he should serve his preceptor with body and mind till studies are over. Thereafter, he should give gurudakṣiṇa to his guru, whatever he can afford, and taking the guru's permission, leave the hermitage. Such a Brahmacāri is known as an Upakūrvāṇa Brahmacāri.

"One who wants to reach Brahmaloka remains a Brahmachāri throughout his life; he is a Naiṣthika Brahmacāri. He should surrender himself to his preceptor and dedicate his whole life to studying the Vedās. He should remain sinless, see the whole world with equanimity, and worship me in all Bhūtās, the soul and the teacher. He will realize that he, his Ātma, his teacher, and the Paramātma, are all one and the same. He should not look at women with lust, touch them or talk to them with love. He should even avoid seeing animals or birds in the act of making love, for even that may arouse his sexual feelings. He should remain clean inside and outside, pray regularly and keep away from tāmasik food and drinks. He should keep his body, mind and words under control, and see God in the entire creation. In this way, a Brāhmin who practises Naiṣthika Brahmacaryaṁ will burn away all tendencies for karmās and become absolutely pure and my perfect bhakta.

After taking leave of his guru, an Upakūrvāṇa Brahmacāri can enter into the next āśraṁ, which is Gārhasthyam. For this, he must marry a suitable woman lesser in age than him, one who is born in the same varṇa or lower varṇās. If he so wishes, skipping Gārhastyam, he can take up Vānaprastha or even Sanyāsa. However, it is better to go from Āśrama to Āśrama in a sequential manner.

Performing yāgās, learning the Vedās etc. should be done by people belonging to the first three varṇās. However, acting as the master of ceremonies and accepting suitable rewards in yāgās and teaching the Vedās can be done only by Brāhmins. They can also earn money by accepting charity. These are the three methods of earning wealth by Brāhmins. If any Brāhmin thinks that accepting charity is not desirable, he can make use of the grains abandoned by the owner or fallen in fields. An ideal Brāhmin will prefer his physical body to be used for penance anyway, for his ultimate aim will be to attain mokṣa. Living frugally but happily in his house without desires and with his mind fixed on me, he will always have peace of mind. I shall rescue those also, who help such poor Brāhmins.

Kings should raise their subjects above miseries, like how parents protect children and the head of elephant herds take care of all the elephants. The king should elevate himself also to higher levels. Such kings, after destroying all evils in this birth, will reach the Indraloka after their death.

If a Brāhmin is not able to live by the prescribed methods,

he can take up the sword like a Kṣatriya or do trading lie a Vaiśya. Similarly, if a Kṣatriya falls on bad times, he can engage in teaching like a Brāhmaṇa or trading like a Vaiśya; he can even hunt for food in extremely bad times. If a Vaiśya gets into financial difficulty, he can serve others like a Śūdra. If a Śūdra gets into financial difficulty, he can earn money through carpentry, weaving mats etc. None should engage in any dishonest job.

During Gārhasthyam, people should perform the Pancayajna, i.e. worship sages by learning Vedās, satisfy ancestors through appropriate rituals, Devās by yāgās, animals by feeding them and guests by receiving them gladly and treating them well. I reside in all of them. Yāgās should be done using wealth earned honestly. While performing them, servants should be treated kindly. A Gṛhasthi should also strive to gradually give up all worldly attractions. The wise know that just like this world, heaven also is mortal. Attachment to family members should be the same as that with unknown people. All are characters in a dream, and will disappear one by one. In this way, the Gṛhasthi should live in his house unattached to his surroundings, without the feeling of ownership of self or others. If he is attached to his family, wealth etc., he will be bound to the material world and will remain ignorant. He will always worry about what will happen to his parents, wife and children once he dies, and will find no peace of mind. Due to such love of family, his mind will always be turbulent; at the time of death also, he will be apprehensive about them. As a result, he will go to hell after death, and later will be born again in this world, not being able to get out of the vicious cycle of births and deaths."

The Lord tells Uddhava about how one should lead the third and fourth āśramās of Vānaprastha and Sanyāsa respectively in the next chapter.

11.18.1-48: "A man who wishes to enter into the Vānaprastha āśram can leave his wife in the care of his children and then proceed to a forest, or he can take her with him. He should wear bark garments and live on fruits and roots obtained from the forest. Roots can be cooked in fire; fruits can be eaten on natural ripening. Grains can be ground on stones. If any guests arrive, they should be fed with whatever he eats. He should not eat meat. As far as possible, he should not store food items or get them from others. He should not cut his hair or nails, should take bath thrice a day, and lie down on the floor.

"In summer, he should do penance standing in the centre of fire, in the rainy season, getting himself drenched fully and in winter, standing neck deep in water. By this, he will learn to ignore dualities and will be able to control his mind. He should follow all rituals as before. By following such a life, he will reach the world attained by Ṛṣis, and later me. If due to advanced age, one starts trembling all over and is not able to continue living such a harsh life in the forest, he can enter into a self-made pyre, all the time fixing his mind on me.

"One who has lost all attraction towards this material world can enter into Sanyāsa. Taking his preceptor's advice and giving up all his properties in charity, he should enter into the Sanyāsa Āśrama, relinquishing all karmās. Devās may lay many obstacles in the path of sanyāsis out of fear and envy. Ignoring all such hindrances, the Sanyāsis should move onward. A man who has taken up sanyās should wear only minimal clothes; he must have a vessel for collecting alms and a short daṇdam or stick for support. He should talk very less or not talk at all at times, sustain his body with minimal needs and control his mind. If these three dandams (disciplines) are not practised, his physical dandam (stick) is of no value.

"He should collect alms from only seven houses a day and be satisfied with it. After coming back, he should wash his hands and feet and eat the food collected in silence, after sharing the same with guests, if any. Totally detached from the world, he should wander about in various villages, towns and cities; mountains and forests etc. enjoying absolute bliss attained due to oneness with me. He will sit in any safe place and contemplate for long on binding and liberation caused by desires and dispassion respectively. Knowing that all that is seen is mortal, he should withdraw totally from the material world, mentally.

"He should believe in the Vedās; should not go against the Śrutis. He should not support anyone indulging in meaningless arguments. A wise sage should not antagonize people and should be able to tolerate even insults from others. He should not sit idle thinking that he will get alms according to his karmas. He should go from house to house to collect his food. He should not become sad on not getting alms or exalt on getting them. He should be content with whatever clothes he gets to wear and whatever sleeping materials he gets to sleep on. He should maintain his exterior and interior clean. He should not differentiate among people as he knows that bodies exist only till death. He is not interested in any worldly pleasure as he is aware that all these ultimately lead to sorrow.

"Some sanyāsis are not sanyāsis in the true sense. They have not controlled their mind and senses; have not shunned materialistic desires and have not developed dispassion. Such people have taken up sanyās only as a method of livelihood. They are in fact cheating the gods, their own souls in which I reside, and dharma in general. They are immature and are deprived of this world and the next.

"The main quality of a sanyāsi is mind-control, while that of a vānaprasthi is contemplation on truth. A gṛhasthi should perform the pancayagyās daily without fail, while a brahmacāri should serve his guru devotedly. All should be devoted to me.

"In this way, in whichever āśram one is, if he does his duties promptly without desirous of the fruits of his actions, if he sees me in everyone and everything, he will develop absolute bhakti. Such a person is unified with me, thereby attaining mokṣa. Hé Uddhava, you asked me how a devotee will become one with the Parabrahmam. This is the answer to that question."

The first seven verses of the next chapter are also spoken by Lord Kṛṣṇa. He says:

11.19.1-7: "One who has realized the ultimate truth gives up everything and takes to sanyāsa. He does not desire anything but me. And I like those who have this knowledge. Gaining true knowledge is superior to penance, pilgrimage, charity, chanting mantrās and so on and so forth. Therefore, Uddhava, know about the ātma comprehensively and serve me in total devotion. The thought that the body, mind and intellect are real is pure imagination, because these were not in existence before birth or after death. Something that does not exist earlier or later cannot exist in the middle also. The notion that these exist in the middle is a creation of Māya. Reality is that only what was present earlier and later is present in the middle also."

Uddhava requests the Lord to elucidate some facts in more detail in the next three ślokās.

11.19.8-10: "Hé master of the universe! And you who have taken the form of the universe! Kindly explain to me in detail that knowledge which is the cause of purity, dispassion, and which is elaborated in the Vedās. To one who is a distressed victim of the miseries of the world, there is no refuge other than you. Please pull out those who have fallen in this dark well of ignorance, and are bitten by the serpent that is Time, by your illuminating words."

Continuing his discourse, Lord Kṛṣṇa said:

11.19.11- 27: "After the great Mahābhārata war, engulfed in remorse due to the death and destruction of relations, teachers and friends in the war, Yudhiṣṭhira approached grand old Bhīṣma to clear his doubts in ethics, religion and spirituality. I was among the many who were witness to this dialogue. One of Yudhiṣṭhira's questions was on the dharmās to be followed for attainment of Mokṣa. I shall relate to you now the answer given by Bhīṣma to Yudhiṣṭhira on such dharmās, like knowledge, dispassion, devotion and the like.

"Knowing that the twenty eight Tatvās or cardinal principles are a manifestation of one, and that the same principle exists in many - this is Jñāna or Parokṣajñāna. (Tatvās, also called Bhāvās are groups of nine, eleven, five and three, totalling twenty eight. Prakṛti, Puruṣa, Mahat-tatva, Ahaṁkāra, and the Panca-Tanmātrās of sight, sound, smell, touch and taste form the first group of nine Tatvās. The next group of eleven Tatvās are the five Jñānendriyās of eyes, ears, nose, skin, and tongue; the five

Karmendriyās of tongue, hands, legs, genitals and anus, and the mind. Next is the group of five Tatvās which are the Panca-Bhūtās of earth, water, fire, air and sky. The last group of three comprise the three Guṇās viz. Satvagṇa, Rajoguṇa and Tamoguṇa.)

"Vijñāna or Aparokṣajñāna is not seeing many and seeing only one. Truth is always present, before the beginning, after the end, and in between. When pride in the body disappears, one gets to know about the self. To come to this level, any one or more of four methods can be tried. These are reading the Vedās, analysing incidents in one's own life, listening to experiences of the enlightened, and logical thinking. The wise should understand that as karmās are mortal, this world, other worlds like the heaven, and even Brahma the creator are mortal, and hence inauspicious.

"Hé Sinless! I have already explained the nature of 'Bhaktiyoga' to you. I shall elaborate the same once more. By having a keen desire to listen to my stories, explaining the same to others, worshipping me by bhajans, happily offering salutations to me, serving my devotees sincerely, being aware that I exist in all bhūtās, performing tasks dear to me like yāgās, havans, vratās, chanting mantrās, enduring physical sufferings, giving alms to the needy, speaking to others in detail about my qualities, dedicating everything to me, giving up all desires, keeping aside cash for works related to me, and so on and so forth, one develops intense love towards me. For him, nothing else matters. As soon as one's mind gets grounded in satvaguṇa, one attains tranquillity, and comes to have absolute faith in me. He develops total detachment from materialism and achieves the ultimate knowledge of the self. If one keeps his mind fixed on his body and family, it runs in all directions and such a person becomes more and more rājasik. He keeps on doing incorrect deeds. Therefore, one should take care to be righteous, see oneself in everyone and everything, develop total dispassion and do only such deeds that enhance one's devotion in me."

At this, Uddhava asked the Lord:

11.19.28-32: "Hé master! Hé destroyer of the wicked! How

many types of yamam and niyamam are there? What are śamam, damam, titikṣa and dhṛti? What are dānam, tapam, śauryam, satyam, ṛtam, tyāgam, iṣtam, dhanam, 'yāgam', and dakṣiṇa? Hé Keśava! What is the strength of a man? What are bhāgyam, lābham, vidya, lajja, śrī, sukham, and duḥkham? Who is a real paṇḍit and who is an absolute mūrkh? Which are the good paths to follow and which are the bad ones to avoid? What are swargam, narakam, and gṛham? Who is a real bandhu? What is the nature of an āḍhyaḥ, a daridraḥ and a kṛpaṇaḥ? Who is Īśwara? Hé Protector of the good people, kindly answer all these questions. Also please enlighten me on the reverses of these."

Lord Kṛṣṇa answered all these questions with great patience.

11.19.33-45: "There are twelve dharmās in yamam and another twelve in niyamam. The former are ahimsa, i.e. not hurting anyone by thought, words or actions; satyam or truthfulness, asteyam, i.e. abstinence from dishonest thoughts and deeds; asanga, i.e. lack of desires; hrī which means sense of shame in doing wrong deeds which leads to not doing them; asanjaya, i.e. not harbouring dreams of yearning; āstikyam, that is belief in the scriptures; brahmacaryam which emphasizes abstinence from sex; maunam which is speaking only when needed; sthairyam, i.e. firm determination to be always righteous; kṣama meaning capacity to endure hardships brought about by one's own karmās, and abhayam, i.e. being brave.

"The latter twelve comprise śaucam, i.e. external and internal cleanliness; japam, i.e. chanting mantrās; tapam or penance, i.e. enduring hardships in the course of worshipping God; homam, i.e. havan; śradha meaning faith in what the scriptures and teachers and elders say; ātithyam meaning hospitality; madarcanam meaning worshipping me; tīrthātanam or pilgrimage; parārthehā meaning willingness to help others; tuṣti or contentment in what one has; and ācāryaseva, i.e. serving one's guru. (As Śaucam is both external and internal, it is counted as two.) Those who follow these yamās and niyamās get whatever they wish for.

"Śamam is fixing one's intellect on me. Damam is indriya-samyamam, i.e. controlling one's senses. Titikṣā is capability to tolerate sorrows while dhṛti is victory over the tongue and the genitals. The most important dānam is not hurting others by shedding one's own tendency to do so. Real tapam is giving up desires. Svabhāva-vijayam, i.e. being of a good disposition is the real śauryam while actual satyam or truth is sama-darśanam, meaning perceiving everyone and everything as equal.

"Ṛtam means words which are true and endearing. Detachment to karmās and absence of ego is the real śaucam, while discarding the desire for the results of karmās is true sanyāsam. Dharmam is that which helps people at all times, in all places. I myself, complete in knowledge and dispassion, am yajña. Instructing true knowledge to others is the real dakṣiṇa. The biggest balam or strength is prāṇāyāmam, i.e. controlling breath, by which a wandering mind can be stabilised.

"Becoming like me is bhāgyam. Perfect lābham is getting to that point where nothing else is required. Vidya is non-discrimination among all that is created. Hree or Lajja is dislike of performing undesirable Karmās. Not craving for anything is Śrī. Saukhyam is remaining above joy and sorrow while craving for materialistic pleasures is Dukkham. A Vidwān is one who knows what Bandha is and what Mokṣa is.

"One who is proud of his body and sense organs is a mūrkh, an ignorant fool. The panthā: or path to me is the right path; it is followed by the stable-minded. The path taken by a wandering mind is a wrong path. Amassing one's satvaguṇa will help one in attaining swarga. Heightening of tamoguṇa is naraka. For anyone, body is only the gṛham or house, for soul is the real self. And I am the bandhu or well-wisher who instructs everyone in this ātmavidya. One who possesses noble qualities is the Dhanika, the real rich man. One who is unhappy is a daridraḥ, i.e. a poor man. And one who has not conquered his indriyās is a kṛpaṇaḥ - a miserable man. An egoless person free of desires is a free man - he is Īśwara. Attachment to desires is contrary to Īśwara-bhāva or godliness.

Hé Uddhava! I have answered all your questions in detail. I have told you the real meanings of all the terms you mentioned.

However, what is the use of knowing all about good qualities and how they differ from bad qualities? Focus on becoming one without any qualities, i.e. discard all Guṇās (sad-guṇās meaning good qualities and dur-guṇās meaning bad qualities). That is the best Guṇa."

In this way, Lord Kṛṣṇa concluded this part of his discourse.

In the next, i.e. the twentieth chapter, we see Uddava as a confused man. In the first five verses, we see him trying to explain to the lord the reason for his confusion. Uddhava also requests Kṛṣṇa to clear his doubts.

11.20.1-5: "Hé lotus-eyed! The difference between the good and the bad are elucidated clearly in the Vedās. The variances among the four Varṇās and the four Āśramās, differences in place, age, time, heaven and hell etc., have been stated unambiguously in the scriptures. You have described to me in detail all that. In fact, it is your own instructions that the Vedās contain. These are guidelines for men and even the Devās. Yet at the end of the entire discourse, you say that there are no differences between them, everything should be considered equally, and seeing things differently is wrong. Please explain why this is so."

The rest of the chapter is wholly devoted to Bhagvān's reply to Uddhava.

11.20.6-38: "I have told you about the three methods by which humans can enhance their real happiness through jñāna or true knowledge, niṣkāma karma or work without desire for benefits, and bhakti, i.e. undiluted devotion. Of these, Jñānayoga is suitable for those who have given up karmās and are dispassionate while Karmayoga is suitable for those who have not yet achieved unabridged detachment. Bhaktiyoga is best for those who are not fully dispassionate, yet are not much attached to materialistic pleasures, and are captivated by my stories and the like. One should perform karmās as long as one feels detached from the worldly ways and develops interest in me.

"Hé Uddhava! The one who is without desires and who does not deviate from his or her dharma never goes to heaven or hell. Such a person who does not deviate from the righteous path, has given up all sinful deeds, and is pure of heart attains knowledge and devotion automatically. Those who are in heaven or hell cannot attain these; it is possible only on this earth. So getting a human birth is most noble. The purpose of this birth is not to attain heaven. Yet people do so because of their ego. The real aim is to strive for salvation through knowledge and devotion. This must be done well before the body falls in death, just like birds living on a tree leave their nests and fly away when they see a woodcutter approach the tree. Realizing that time is gnawing away at one's life incessantly, one should give up all affection to the mortal body and know the soul.

"The physical body is like a boat on the ocean of the materialistic world. It has the advantage of having a guru as the boatman, and me as the supportive wind. Yet, if this ship is not able to cross the ocean, it is most unfortunate. When a yogi becomes disinterested in karmās as well as their consequences, he, with constant practice, is able to fix his mind on me. Whenever the mind wavers, it must be brought back with the help of intellect. This must be done without getting demoralised. Controlling the mind in this way is the noblest yoga. Such a person will understand everything about the universe, its creation and dissolution. He can then easily meditate on me.

"A yogi who is detached himself from the external world in totality becomes perfect; he does not do anything wrong. He is always interested in performing good karmas and avoiding bad ones. Moreover, if he does do something wrong by mistake, his yoga itself is capable of burning away that sin.

"A devotee is very much interested in me. However, he may not be able to give up karmās entirely despite knowing them to be distractions. So he must pray to me, knowing very well that karmās are the cause of sorrow. As I sit in the heart of true devotees, worldly desires in them are gradually destroyed. On seeing me, all his doubts are cleared and all his karmās vanish. Such a devotee does not need knowledge about the universe or practise of detachment from it. As a result of his absolute devotion, he will get whatever he wishes for, be it Swarga,

Mokṣa, Vaikuṇṭha or anything else. In short, Bhaktiyoga takes one to the pinnacle of bliss. However, true bhaktās do not desire even mokṣa, which is the liberation from the cycle of births and deaths. They develop 'Nairapekṣya'; i.e. they do not wish for anything. They want only bhakti in me. My absolute devotees, who are stable minded, and have experienced the Ātman which is different from Buddhi, are not affected by the consequences of good or bad deeds. They come to know what parabraḥmam is and attain my loka which is free of fear."

Here, the twentieth chapter of the eleventh canto ends. All the forty three ślokās of the next chapter are spoken by Lord Kṛṣṇa.

11.21.1-43: "Some do not follow any of the three pathways of bhakti, jñāna or karma which lead to me; instead, they follow the diktat of their senses and are forever unsatisfied with their lives. The goodness or badness of deeds varies for different people and for different situations. For example, when one is attacked, he can retaliate. But when there is no such danger, one should not attack others. Thus, the same deed may bring guṇa or doṣa to the doer. Differentiating between guṇa and doṣa is not absolute; it is subjective.

"Just like deeds, things also may be good or bad. Snake venom can kill a man; it can also save a man from death if used as a medicine in an appropriate situation. Fresh food is good while stale food is bad. There are many such examples. To remove badness or dirt from some things, other things or procedures are used. Drying in the sun, washing in water or oil, heating, boiling in water, burning in fire etc. are all practised in different cases. Removing dirt from unclean things to make them clean again is called śaucam.

"Places also can be good or bad. For example, places where there is no respect for learned Brahmaṇās is a bad place. A place which is not kept clean is also bad. Time during which good deeds are done is good; time when good deeds are not done or cannot be done due to obstacles is bad. Attributing goodness or badness of actions, things, places etc. is all meant for implementation of Dharma.

"The Pancabhūtās of which the whole universe is made affect different things differently. Performing good deeds and remembering me cleanses the mind. One's deeds should be always beneficial for the world. A mantra becomes pure when the one who chants it knows its meaning correctly. In short, where place, time, material, doer, mantra and karma are pure, dharma manifests itself.

"Dharma, i.e. righteousness or morality, removes ignorance and fear and provides humans joy and peace of mind. Attraction to materialistic objects leads to desires. When these are not fulfilled, one becomes angry and loses the power of reasoning. Such a person is unable to differentiate the good from the bad; the physical from the spiritual. He lives, breathing in and out, but his life has no purpose.

"Such people, who are ignorant, are not able to interpret the scriptures correctly. In the Vedās, the meanings of some verses are hidden. It is like a father telling his son that if he takes a particular medicine, he will be given a sweetmeat. The real purpose is to cure the disease; eating the sweetmeat is just an offshoot of the whole process.

"Right from birth, everyone is interested in satisfying the senses. As years progress, he or she gets more and more engrossed in such activities. They grow up not knowing the real truth. Such ignorant people give more importance to the 'phalaśrutis' at the end of prayer songs, describing the worldly benefits that would ensue from the singing of these songs. The ignorant, the lustful, and the greedy mistake flowers for fruits, and perform various deeds, but none of them know that I reside within them. They conduct yagyās, even sacrificing animals, and try to propitiate various Devās and the spirits of ancestors through such procedures, in the hope of becoming prosperous in this world and, after death, going to heaven. Such people, who do not understand the real meaning of the Vedās, do not even wish to know me. They are not able to break out of the birth-death cycle.

"The Vedās are deep like an ocean. One is not able to

comprehend the essence of the Vedās easily. However, what they proclaim is that this whole world is an illusion; Braḥmam is the only reality and that is the same as Ātma. Ṛṣis declare the same, but indirectly. I like the indirect method too, because I would like humans to contemplate and analyse each and every fact. I am that Braḥmam, with infinite power. I exist as the primordial sound of 'Aum' in all Bhūtās. From this, letters and words originate. All these dissolve back in me too. The exact meaning of the letters and words is known only to me. I am the ultimate goal of whatever method one chooses to follow – jñāna mārgam, karma mārgam or bhakti mārgam. Nothing else matters."

The Lord concluded his speech thus. And here ends the twenty first chapter. At the beginning of the next chapter, we see Uddhava seeking clarification from Lord Kṛṣṇa regarding the exact number of the Cardinal Principles, in three ślokās.

11.22.1-3: "Hé Master of the Universe! Hé Lord! Some time back, you said that the Tatvās or the Cardinal Principles are twenty eight in number. However, different Ṛṣis have given varying views on the number of these principles. Why are they doing so?"

The Lord replied:

11.22.4-25: "The enlightened Ṛṣis know what Braḥmam is and as such there are no discrepancies in what they say. However, if any of them insists that only he is right, that is because of my māya. When they achieve śamam and damam, all differences disappear. The Principles manifest as many; they can be classified differently and made into different number of groups accordingly. Hence, one can consider all opinions to be true. For example, Jīvan and Puruṣan can be considered to be two. As ultimately, they are one and the same, they can be counted as one also. In the same way, the Tatvās can be counted differently by different permutation combinations of the twenty eight basic Principles. The whole universe is formed from these Principles, in different groupings, with the power of Prakṛti, under the observation of Īśwara.

"All calculations are right in their own way, as all have their own reasons. For example, those who opine that the Cardinal Principles are seventeen in number count Bhūtās, Indriyās and Tanmātrās as five each, totalling fifteen, the sixteenth being Manas, and the seventeenth one Ātma. Those who believe the Principles as sixteen include Manas and Ātma together as one entity. Some include the five Bhūtās and the five Indriyās, along with Manas, Jīvātma and Paramātma, making it a group of thirteen Cardinal Principles.

"Some believe that the Principles are eleven in number and they include the five Bhūtās, the five Indriyās and the Ātma. Here, Jīvan and Manas are included in the Ātma. According to some, there are just nine Principles, and these are the eight Prakṛtis and the single Puruṣa. There are some more totals, based on various variations and groupings. Therefore, one should not worry about the differences seen in the interpretations by the different Ṛṣis. If you contemplate on these various views and analyse them well, you will see that all are logical."

Uddhava said:

11.22.26-28: "Hé Kṛṣṇa! Though Prakṛti and Puruṣa are different in nature, they have no apparent differences as they are dependent on each other. How does Prakṛti exist in Puruṣa or the Ātma and vice versa? Hé lotus-eyed! You are all knowing, and so can easily clear my doubts. Jīvās get knowledge from your power. And only you know how your Māya works."

Bhagvān Kṛṣṇa clears his friend's doubts in five verses:

11.22.29-33: "Hé noble one! Apparently, Prakṛti is different from Puruṣa. The former is formed by the blending of all Guṇās. This is made possible by my Māya. The Indriyās, or the sense organs, and their corresponding senses work in unison with the mind. Differences occur when the three Guṇās stand out separately due to the action of Ahaṁkāra or ego. Debate on whether Ātma or Puruṣa is different from Prakṛti does not make any sense, in reality. Yet this debate will remain alive among the ignorant and will continue for ever."

At this juncture, Uddhava makes a request to the Lord in two verses.

11.22.34-35: "Hé Lord! How do the ignorant and those not interested in you get different bodies and leave these bodies based on their own karmās? Govinda! Kindly reveal to me this truth, which is not known to such people. There is none in this world who knows this truth."

Lord Kṛṣṇa gives an elaborate reply to this question put forward by Uddhava. This comprises the rest of this entire chapter, except the last two ślokās.

11.22.36-58: "Mind is the master of all the indriyās. It creates its own different states of mind. The mind can create anything while the body is awake or asleep. At the time of death, the subtle body of humans including mind move from one world to another; the Jīvan follows the mind. With death, the memory power of the mind vanishes. It regains its memory power on taking birth again. In other words, the mind in the new body does not remember anything about the previous body it was occupying. The Jīvan in this body thinks that it is his own, falling a prey to Ahaṁkāra. Like the mind, Jīvan also cannot recollect the desires or anything else the old body had. In fact, the loss of memory of the mind and the Jīvan is death of the body. Similarly, birth is receiving a new body, which, again the Jīvan considers its own. Thus, death takes place only of the body.

"Bhūtās are formed and are dissolved every fraction of a second, i.e. birth and death of cells are taking place incessantly in the body. However, as time flies faster, these changes are not visible. A flame lives for a microsecond only; what we see the next moment is another flame. Similarly, in flowing water, the water that we see in one moment is different from what we see in the next moment. Same is the case of the human body. The cells that make up his body differ from moment to moment. Thus, just like the thought that "This is the same flame" or "This is the same flowing water", the thought that "This is the same body" is also wrong. The body is mortal; it dies and is reborn repeatedly while the Jīvan does not die. It is ignorance to think that Jīvan is born when a body is formed and it dies when the body dies. Fire is always there; but it manifests itself only when firewood is burnt. Similar is the case of the Jīvan. It does not die, neither is it born.

"A body goes through nine states – entering the womb, growth in the womb, birth, infanthood, childhood, youth, middle age, old age and death. As Jīvan considers the body to be his, he also believes that he goes through these nine states. This is because of unification with the Guṇās. This misunderstanding of the Jīvan clears up on getting God's blessings.

"A person is not aware of his or her own body at the time of birth or death. These two phenomena are known only because one does the necessary rituals after his father's death and does the required rituals for his new born child. The all-knowing Ātma is aware of the fact that the body is born and that it dies while it is immortal.

"One sees the germination of a seed, the growth of the sapling into a tree, formation of flowers and fruits on it, and the ultimate death of the tree after a few years. An enlightened man understands that his body also goes through similar stages from birth to death; so he is not affected by these changes. He knows that Jīvan is different from the body. It does not have these states of birth, development and death.

"An ignorant person cannot differentiate Prakṛti from Ātma, and embroiled in desires, remains attached to the world. Those people who possess Satvaguṇa and do good karmās become Ṛṣis or Devās. Those in whom Rajoguṇa is dominant become human beings or asurās. Those people who show over-riding Tamoguṇa take birth as plants or other creatures.

"Due to the fine waves in a pond, reflections of trees at its bank also quiver. Just like this, the experiences of the senses are also not real. The Ātman does not experience any of these. All that a person perceives through his sense organs are unreal, just like the characters and events in a dream. Yet, as he thinks that his experiences are real, joys and sorrows arising out of these experiences also look real to him.

Therefore, hey Uddhava! Understand that joys and sorrows will vanish when one gets ātmajñāna, i.e. knowledge of the true self. Even if one is insulted and humiliated by wicked people, or is envied by them, or is physically assaulted or even spat or urinated upon, if he wishes to have permanent happiness, he should raise his soul using his intellect."

At this, Uddhava said:

11.22.59-60: "Hé All-knowing! Only those who have surrendered themselves to you wholly can be like this. I personally feel that it is most difficult to endure boundless physical and mental assaults. Human nature will not allow any normal person to go through such battering. Hé noblest among teachers! Kindly explain this in a simple understandable way."

Here ends the twenty second chapter. The next chapter starts with a śloka by Maharṣi Śuka, who was reciting and explaining the great Śrīmad Bhāgavat Purāṇ composed by his father Sage Vedavyāsa to King Parīkṣit during his last week on Earth.

11.23.1: "When Uddhava, the noblest among bhaktās, requested Śrī Kṛṣṇa, capable of removing the sins of others and purifying their minds, for an explanation, the latter began his discourse heartily.

The Lord began:

11.23.2-5: Hé Bṛhaspati's disciple! Physical pain is much less when compared to mental pain. There is none in this world great enough to endure the pain from wounds caused by wicked people's hurting words. I shall now describe to you an incident in this context. Listen carefully. It is the story of a Sanyāsi, who, remembering his past, sang this song."

This song is famous as the Bhikṣugīta. It has been dealt with in Chapter Twelve of this book. The Gīta itself extends from Verse 43 to Verse 58 of this chapter. At first, Lord Kṛṣṇa elaborates in a few verses the past life of the Brāhmin, who becomes a Bhikṣu later.

11.23.6-42: "In the land of Avanti, there lived a rich, miserly Brāhmin. He made a lot of money from his many businesses as well as farming, yet was always greedy. He was short tempered and was least hospitable to guests who happened to visit his home. Members of his family and the servants were very sad and angry at his cruelty towards them. Gradually, they began disobeying and ignoring him. Over time, he lost all his riches. Some was taken away by relatives, some was stolen by thieves, some was lost through natural calamities, some went to the royal treasury through fines etc., and the rest just withered away as time passed. Finally, when he became a pauper, everyone left him and went away. At this juncture, he remembered his earlier deeds. He regretted all that he had done and realized how wicked he was. He understood how foolish he had been, working hard to amass wealth that ultimately led to his downfall. He cried pitiably and began analysing his past life. As he did so, he became wise.

"He thought, 'The wealth I created was not used for righteous purposes. People like me do not experience any happiness in this life. Neither will they be happy after death, as they are sure to go to hell. Wealth always leads to unhappiness. One has to go through great difficulties in earning it, accumulating it, spending it properly, saving it etc. On top of this, one feels terribly sad when he loses it. Thus riches make men stressful, scared, sad, apprehensive, deceitful, greedy, angry, arrogant, foolish, competitive, distrustful, intolerant, miserable, discriminatory, and hurtful. People develop these fifteen bad qualities when they love wealth.

'Even parents, siblings, wife, children, and friends become enemies and fight with one another for even small amounts of money. In the process, all hurt each other. Despite being born as human beings and that too, as honourable Brāhmins, some engage in wrong deeds and waste their life away. Should anyone, after getting a human body which can be used to enter swarga or even attain mokṣa, be attracted to riches, the seat of all misery, knowing fully well of the mortality of the body? Yet there are many who yearn for riches, and on getting the same, enjoy it themselves, and also give part thereof to gods, sages and own family and friends. Not satisfied with this, they desire for more riches. Such people, whose desire is insatiable, go to hell after death.

'In my case, I just worked hard to earn money and did not care to spend it properly either. Now I have become old and weak. How can I do any physical work now? Even some wise men lead lives like me, working hard to earn money and then face all sorts of troubles. There is certainly something which binds people in a web of māya. Everyone has to die one day leaving all his wealth behind and be born again. What then is the use of all this?

'I am sure that Bhagvān Viṣṇu is pleased with me, for He has made me dispassionate like this. He has provided me with this boat of detachment to cross the ocean of materialism easily. If I have some more years left, I shall be careful and spend my time in praying to God. Let the gods be pleased with me. Long ago, Khaṭvāngan was liberated in a moment. I can also attain liberation like him.'

"With this firm determination, the old Brāhmin discarded thoughts of 'I' and 'mine', gave up all desires and became a Bhikṣu. Having controlled his mind, Indriyās and Prāṇa by dispassion and yoga, he wandered in unknown villages and towns collecting alms. Seeing the old and unkempt Bhikṣu, wicked people troubled him in many ways.

"Despite all this, as he was an absolute sātvik now, he was in total control of his senses. Taking all these various types of tortures to be the consequences of his bad Karmās, the Bhikṣu was unmoved, and roamed about singing."

This is the Bhikṣugītam, comprising the next sixteen verses. (11.23.43-58). These verses have been explained in Chapter Twelve of this book.

Concluding the story of the Bhikṣu in this way, Lord Kṛṣṇa told Uddhava,

11.23.59-62: "Thus, after losing all his wealth, family and friends, the Brāhmin became a sage. Thereafter, bearing all the torture and insults heaped on him by others, he remained stable-minded and sang this Bhikṣugīta. It is not others that give joy or sorrow to anyone. It is because of ignorance that one sees another as a friend or a foe or someone indifferent to his affairs. It is all in the mind. Therefore, fix your intellect in me and conquer your mind. This is the gist of yoga. Whoever listens to this Bhikṣugītam, understands it, sings it for others, triumphs over his mind, and is never affected by joys and sorrows. He becomes a sthitaprajña, tranquil in mind at all times, in all situations."

All the twenty nine ślokās of the next chapter are spoken by the Lord. In the first twenty, he describes the real nature of Brahmam.

11.24.1-20: "I shall now explain to you Sāṁkhyam, one of the many Śāstrās. Once you understand Sāṁkhya Śāstra fully, all your confusions will vanish. Even before creation, Brahmam—singular, indivisible, indestructible and which cannot be subject to mind and words—was always there. Before Kṛtayuga also, everything occurring in the universe did exist, but in a subtle form, having no name or form. In the Kṛtayuga, the truly intelligent people knew this fact. It was that Brahman itself that divided into the visible and the subtle – the visible was the dṛśyam, i.e. Prakṛti and the subtle, the Puruṣa. Prakṛti got its three Guṇās of satvam, rajas and tamas because of its association with the Puruṣa. From the Guṇās, mahattatvam or the capability to know (Jñānasakti) and ability to function (Kriyāsakti) originated. Mahattatvam gave rise to Ahaṁtatvam. As the Guṇās are three in number, Ahaṁtatvam, sometimes referred to as Ahaṁkāra also, is also of three types. From Tāmasik Ahaṁtatvam, Tanmātrās, i.e. senses were formed. The associations among the five senses of sound, touch, form, taste and smell gave rise to the Pancabhūtās or the five elements – ākāśam (sky), vāyu (air), agni (fire), jalam (water) and bhūmi (earth). From Rājasik Ahaṁkāra, the ten Indriyās (five Jñānendriyās and five Karmenndriyās) and Antaḥkaraṇa originated. Devās controlling these eleven entities were created from Sātvik Ahaṁkāra.

"All these tatvās, as per my wish, joined together to form the primordial symbolic aṇḍam or egg. In the flood waters, in which everything was dissolved, did this egg lay. I entered this egg in the form of Nārāyaṇa. From my navel originated a lotus containing all the subtle matter of the past and future, named the Universe. Lord Brahma was formed in this lotus flower. After a very prolonged penance, Brahma in whom rajoguṇa became dominant by my blessing, created three entities – bhūlokam or the world, swargalokam or the heaven and bhuvarlokam or the atmosphere in between. Bhūlokam became the residing place of humans and other creatures, Swargalokam that of Devās and Bhuvarlokam came to be occupied by the spirits. In addition to these three, a separate loka by name Maharlokam also was created by Brahma for Maharṣīs like Bhṛgu and Siddhas. For Asurās and Nāgās, he created the Saptalokās including Atala etc. Yogīs and Sanyāsīs, due to their saintly karmās, go to Maharloka, Janarloka, Tapoloka, Satyaloka etc. However, those who are true devotees of me, attain my loka, which is Vaikuṇṭha. Only they can overcome the cycle of births and deaths and be unified with me.

"Creatures perform different karmās because of their different Guṇās and go up and down as a consequence. Yet the single Ātma exists in all and pervades the whole universe. The smallest to the largest matter in the universe has resulted from the union of Prakṛti and Puruṣa, which has originated from Brahmam. Ultimately, Brahmam is the only truth. It is the same in past, present and future. When earth, i.e. mud, is made into a pot, it still remains earth. When the pot breaks, what is left is also earth. The cause and the effect are not different from one another. In the beginning, Brahmam was the reason for creation. In the middle, various living and non-living things were formed. In the end, everything will dissolve in the Brahmam. Creation, preservation and dissolution go on as long as Brahmam exists."

The last nine verses are about the real meaning of Pralayam or Deluge. The Lord continues:

11.24.21-29: "All creation, with their different forms and functions, dissolve in me, manifesting as the Pancabhūtās, i.e. the five elements only, from which they were originally formed. In fact, it is this dissolution that is known as Pralayam or the final deluge. This takes place step by step. The sequence of this dissolution is just the opposite of that of creation. For example, plants were formed from the earth, food was formed from the plants and body was formed from food. If there is no food, there is no body – so the body disbands in food. Similarly, food dissolves in plants and plants in earth. Earth gets unified with smell, which dissolves in water. In this order, next is taste, fire, form, air, touch, sky, and sound. All these were formed from Tāmasāhaṁkāra. Finally, sound becomes one with Tāmasāhaṁkāra.

"Now I shall tell you what happens to the Indriyās formed from Rājasāhaṁkāra. They dissolve in the Devātās who are their masters, and finally all become one with Rājasāhaṁkāra. The seat of all, which is the manass or the mind is unified with Sātvikāhaṁkāra. All the three Ahaṁkārās dissolve in Mahattatvam, which is unified with Guṇās, which in turn disbands in Prakṛti, and Prakṛti in endless Time. Time gets amalgamated with Jīvan, and Jīvan with Ātma. As Ātma is not different from Paramātma or Brahmam, it exists in itself. And I am that Brahman.

"If one understands clearly the sequence of creation and dissolution, he or she will realize that though many objects appear to exist in the universe, ultimately all are one and the same. That there are many objects is a wrong impression created by the mind. Clearing this misunderstanding takes one from the darkness of ignorance to the light of knowledge. This is just like how the rising sun removes darkness and spreads light everywhere.

"Understanding of Sāṁkhya abolishes all doubts in one's mind as he comes to know the cause and effect of whatever exists in the universe, and 'anulomam', i.e. the order in which they are created, and 'pratilomam', i.e. the order in which they are finally dissolved. I have thus told you the gist of the Sāṁkhya Śāstra."

All the thirty six Ślokās of the next chapter are spoken by Bhagvān Śrī Kṛṣṇa.

11.25.1-11: "Hé noble hearted! I shall now tell you how association with the three Guṇās affects the nature of different people. Listen and understand. Characteristics resulting from satvaguṇa are victory over indriyās, patience, contemplation on philosophy, treading the righteous path at all times, truthfulness, kindness, memory, happiness, selflessness, detachment from materialism, respect towards teachers and scriptures, humility, charitable disposition, contentment etc. Behavioural patterns resulting from rajoguṇa are desire for worldly pleasures, pride, dissatisfaction, differential treatment of others, lust, fighting nature, enjoying flattery, making fun of others, showing off of heroism, exhibiting strength etc. Tamoguṇa leads to characters like intolerance, miserliness, fraudulence, tendency to fight with others, hurtfulness, lethargy, dissatisfaction, confusion, greed, fear, boastfulness, laziness etc.

"These are the characters resulting from the three Guṇās. Now I shall tell you what happens due to mixing of these Guṇās. Hé Uddhava! Thoughts of 'I' and 'mine' result from the admixing of Guṇās. A person with mixed Guṇās will believe in Śāstrās and will lead a good householder's life, along a righteous path. In those who worship me with their deeds, without desire for the fruits thereof, satvaguṇa is dominant. In those who worship me, desirous of materialistic pleasures, rajoguṇa is dominant. Those who worship me with intentions of hurting others are tāmasik in nature."

11.25.12-23: "All the three Guṇās originate in the mind, which is an aspect of Jīvan. While Jīvan is subject to Guṇās, I am not. Satvaguṇa is bright, pure, and serene. When this guṇa is dominant over the other two, the person who possesses it will become more knowledgeable, and righteous. When Rajoguṇa dominates the other two, the person will aspire for wealth, name and fame; failure to achieve these will lead to sorrow. On Tamoguṇa overriding the first two, wisdom is lost and laziness increases. This leads to fear, sorrow, longing, violence, tendency to hurt others etc.

"Know that Satvaguṇa, where I reside, becomes primary when the mind becomes peaceful, the indriyās stop craving, fear of death of the body vanishes, and an overall absence of desires sets in. If you see a person feeling happy or sad due to the successes or failures resulting from his actions, who is restless on account of his intellect and senses being active at all times, and whose mind is confused, know that he is rājasik by nature. Understand that one whose intellect is not capable of grasping facts, whose mind is incapable of rising to heights, who is ignorant, and gloomy is tāmasik.

"When satvaguṇa is prominent, Devās become powerful, when rajoguṇa exceeds, asurās become powerful and when tamoguṇa dominates, rakṣases take command. Similarly, when one is awake, that is, when he is in the jāgṛtāvastha, it is satvaguṇa that dominates; when he is dreaming, i.e. when he is in the swapnāvastha, rajoguṇa is dominant and when one is in dreamless slumber, that is, in a state of suṣupti, it is tamoguṇa that is foremost in him. When a person is existing in all these three states, and is witness to all the three at all times, he is said to be in a state of turīya – this is the fourth avastha or state.

"It is depending on the Guṇās that upward and downward movement of living beings takes place. Thus, sātvik people become Brahmins and rise high up on the ladder to reach satyaloka. Tāmasik people fall lower and lower and take birth even as immovable trees etc. People who are in between, with a rājasik nature, remain as human beings, engrossed in work at all times. Those who die when Satvaguṇa is dominant in them attain swarga. Those who die when rajoguṇa is overriding continue being in the world of humans and those who die when tamoguṇa is at its peak in them reach hell. Those who are above all the three types of Guṇās are unified with me. Deeds which are done without desire for fruits, and which are dedicated to me, originate from satvaguṇa; deeds done with desire for their fruits originate in rajoguṇa, and those done with the aim of hurting others, have their origin in tamoguṇa."

11.25.24-27: "Knowledge about mokṣa is a product of satvaguṇa; knowledge that differentiates one from another is a result of rajoguṇa, and that which prevails at only the base level results from tamoguṇa. Only those who are beyond any guṇa obain unqualified knowledge about me. When Satvaguṇa is dominant, people like to live in forests; when rajoguṇa is dominant, they prefer to live in towns or villages; and when tamoguṇa peaks, they like to spend time in gambling dens or other such places of vice. Those who have reached a state beyond Guṇās will prefer to live in temples or other holy places. When satvaguṇa is in excess, one prefers to be with me alone and hence shuns other company; one in whom rajoguṇa is superfluous is blind with materialistic desires and one with excessive tamoguṇa is ignorant. One who is beyond Guṇās has shed all arrogance and depends on me at all times. Interest in and respect to Vedās and Śāstrās is because of satvaguṇa; interest in Yāgās and other such Karmās results from rajoguṇa, and, attraction to and involvement in adharma or bad deeds are consequences of tamoguṇa. Those beyond Guṇās are keen only in serving me."

11.25.28-29: "Sātviks will prefer to eat simple, pure, and easily available food like vegetables, fruits etc. When rajoguṇa governs, one would like to satiate his senses with spicy food, and when tamoguṇa is in control, unclean and unhealthy food, which causes hurt, is preferred. Happiness due to contentment originates from satvaguṇa; happiness due to fulfilling of desires of the sense organs originates from rajoguṇa, and that obtained from intoxicating objects has its foundation in tamoguṇa. Pleasure on dedicating everything to me is caused by being in a state beyond Guṇās. In short, everything in this world is caused by the relative ascendancy of the three Guṇās whose seat is the mind."

11.25.30-36: "Matter, place, experience, time, knowledge, karma and kārmik, respect, form, state of being – in short, everything exists because of the three Guṇās. In fact, all that is seen or heard, all that is understood by intelligence – all originate due to union of Prakṛti and Puruṣa and are variations of Guṇās. These Guṇās, which originate from the mind, should be won over. If true devotees, residing in me because of bhaktiyoga, want to become one with me, they should become wise, shun all the three Guṇās, conquer their senses, get detached from all materialistic longings, and worship me. For this, they should win over rajoguṇa and tamoguṇa first, and finally satvaguṇa also, by controlling the mind. When this happens, Jīvan leaves the sūkṣma-śarīr or the subtle body, of which it is a part, and becomes one with me, i.e. brahma. At this stage, Jīvan is not different from Brahman. It is now a Jīvanmukta."

In the next, i.e. the twenty-sixth chapter of the eleventh canto of Śrīmad Bhāgavatam, Bhagvān continues explaining the philosophy of the Sanātana Dharma to Uddhava.

11.26.1-3: "Having obtained this human body, one who worships me constantly attains me, i.e. the Paramātma, residing in the Ātma in the form of ultimate bliss. He knows that though he is in a human body, all this is mere illusion, and so he is dispassionate at all times. One should avoid the company of those who live only to satisfy their sense organs, for it is like a blind man taking the help of another blind man to walk – both may fall into a pit. Similarly, the wise can be misguided by the ignorant."

At this juncture, Lord Kṛṣṇa tells Uddhava the story of King Purūravas and the apsara Urvaśi. Rendering of this story is done in twenty two verses – from 11.26.4 to 11.26.25. These verses have been explained in the thirteenth chapter of this book, captioned Ailagīta.

The Lord continues his narration to Uddhava from the next verse onwards till the end of the twenty sixth chapter of the eleventh canto of Śrīmad Bhāgavatam. He says:

11.26.26-34: "Therefore, the wise shun bad company and mingle with virtuous people, who draw them away from worldly desires. The virtuous are those who have fixed their minds in me, who are at peace, see all as equals without discrimination, are not proud, and have given up all worldly desires. They will be constantly immersed in my thoughts and will happily narrate my stories to all those who are willing to listen. Those listeners who are attentive, become my devotees and are then absolved of their sins. For them, who love me unconditionally, what else is there to wish for? One who lights a fire is freed of cold, darkness and fear. In the same way, one who keeps the company of the wise become fearless, as all their ignorance is burnt away. For those who are drowning in an ocean, a boat becomes a savior. In the same way, the wise who know Brahman remove sorrows caused by ignorance. Like how food gives strength, the wise give courage. When the sun removes darkness, the external eyes can see objects. Similarly, knowledgeable people give light to the internal eyes with which the truth about the self can be seen. In this, there is no difference between them and me.

11.26.35: "When truth dawned on him, Purūravas became a wise man. He gave up the thought of Urvaśi and all other worldly desires, and roamed the earth in absolute bliss."

Here ends the twenty sixth chapter. In the next chapter, which is a long one comprising fifty five verses, the first five verses are spoken by Uddhava. He says:

11.27.1-5: "Hé protector of devotees! Please explain to me the intricacies of kriyāyoga. I would like to know which devotees worship you by what all means. Great sages like Nārada, Vedavyāsa, Angiras and many others have stated that worship of God is the noblest deed that man can perform. You had told Brahma that worshipping you leads to mokṣa. The Creator had told this to his sons like Maharṣi Bhṛgu. Śrī Parameśwara described to Devi Pārvati the methodology of your worship. I think that this is the best method for all – men and women, of all castes and ages, to attain liberation. Hé lotus-eyed! Hé master of masters! Kindly tell this devotee of yours in detail how to worship you. By practicing it, I can get out of this birth and death cycle."

Bhagvān complies with Uddhava's request. He elaborates in great detail the procedure to be followed in worshipping Viṣṇu.

11.27.6-22: "The ways of worshipping me are infinite. I shall tell you about them briefly. Pūja may be done basically in three ways – Vedic, tantric or mixed. One can follow any of these methods. Pūja should be done single-mindedly, with devotion, to idols, or on the ground, in water, fire or to the sun or one's guru, or in one's own heart. The aim should be to become dispassionate. Before starting, body and mind should be cleansed.

Idols are of different types. Some are made of materials like stone, wood, metals, sand or gems. Drawings or paintings may be made on the ground or walls using sandalwood paste, kumkum paste etc. Idols may also be imaginary, given form in the mind. In this manner, idols can be of eight types. They may be permanent, as those fixed in temples, or they may be temporary as pictures drawn with sandal paste. Depending on the material used to make the idol, they can be washed or just wiped. Pūja can be done with flowers and various types of offerings. If the whole process is done mentally, everything should be imagined.

Only if the Pūja is done on idols, pouring milk, water etc. on them and decorating them with ornaments need be done. If the puja is done in water, milk, flowers etc. can be used. If it is a havan, ghee should be used along with other offerings put in the fire. Performing puja with water, flowers, incenses, sweets etc. makes me happy. However, I shall be equally content with just water, if the offering is done with absolute bhakti. The articles needed should be collected beforehand, and placed nearby. Then, sit comfortably, facing east or north. Remove the previous day's flowers etc. and then wipe the idol neatly. Mix flowers, sandalwood paste etc. in the water to be used, kept in three vessels. The substances to be put in the three differ, like raw rice, kumkum, durwa grass, sesame, mustard etc., in addition to specific flowers, as instructed in the various Śāstrās. Sprinkle a little of this water on the idol, the site itself, and on the self. Utter suitable mantras and the Gāyatri for each vessel.

11.27.23-31: "Thereafter, do prāṇāyāma and then meditate on one's own Ātma. When I manifest within the worshipper, this power can be transferred to the idol. Imagine me sitting in the centre of a lotus with eight petals, surrounded by various shaktis and the sun, moon, and fire. Worship my weapons like the chakra, conch, mace, sword, bow and arrows etc. Then, worship other signs like Kaustubham, Śrīvatsam, floral garland etc. on my chest. Worship the gods of the eight directions and my followers on the eight sides and Garuda at the back. If affordable, mix fragrant materials like saffron, sandalwood powder, raw camphor, khus khus etc. in the water used for my abhiṣekam or sacred bathing. Chant my names and utter suitable mantras.

11.27.32-35: "Decorations for my idol can be clothes,

sandalwood paste, jewels, garlands of tulsi etc. After puja with flowers, raw rice mixed with turmeric powder, kummum etc., and arati with incense, lamp and camphor, sweets and snacks can be offered to me. If the devotee is rich, he can offer sweets made with rice, milk, ghee, sugar or jiggery, grated coconut and salty snacks made with rice flour, butter and salt etc. every day. Otherwise, such offerings need be made only on special days. Similarly, giving the idol special oil bath, offering sweets of various types, arranging bhajans and dance etc. may be done daily or on special days only."

11.27.36-49: "Those who wish to have more results can worship me by performing yāgās. A yāga is an offering in fire. First of all, a specific place should be cleaned thoroughly, and a pit for lighting the fire should be prepared. There are specifications about the size of this homa-kunda, which a guru can tell the worshipper. After lighting the fire, the flames scattered in different areas within the kunda should be gathered in the centre with hands and later with dry Dūrva leaves. After sprinkling holy water on it, offerings should be deposited in the fire, using a long wooden spoon called Udharaṇi. With each offering, after the mantra, the word 'Swāha', meaning 'well said', is to be uttered. The worshipper should meditate on me in the centre of the fire.

"I must be visualized as a peaceful figure shining like molten gold, carrying a conch, disc, mace and lotus in my four hands, wearing a silk robe whose colour is that of the pollen of a lotus flower, a glittering crown, various ornaments of gold and gems, the divine gem Kaustabham on my neck and the scar Śrīvatsam on my chest, the long floral garland hanging from neck to knees. Meditating on this form of mine, clean dry twigs (samith) dipped in ghee should be put into the fire. Some ghee should be poured into the fire along with. Uttering the required mantras, the concerned God and the Fire God should be worshipped.

"On the conclusion of the homam, meditate on me, manifestation of the Brahmam, and chant the basic mantra. Then, prostrate yourself before the homa-kunda. Deliberate that the Supreme Being and the Fire God have finished having the food and water offered. Then, do Ācamanam by sipping the holy water thrice. Dedicate the remaining offerings to Viṣwaksena, my Commander-in-Chief, and envisage him partaking of it.

"Once the puja and homam are over, singing bhajans in different languages, dancing to them, acting out incidents in my life, reading sacred books to others etc. are all very good practices. These should be done leisurely, without any hurry. After this, prostrate yourself before God, praying for his blessings. Touch your head to my feet, clasp them with both hands reverently, and pray for liberation from the fear of death. Then, take flowers from His feet, believing that He is giving you these flowers, and wear them on your head with devotion. If divinity has been invoked into a temporary idol using one's own inner energy, the same should be taken out and absorbed back after the puja. Idols of all types are equally revered. I am omnipresent. As such, I exist in all idols.

"This is Kriyāyoga, the method of worshipping me. It is called so as it elaborates the various methods to be adopted, as per the Vedās, during Pūja, Yāga etc. A devotee who worships me adopting any of these methods, gets the results he wishes for in this world and the next."

11.27.50-55: "The wealthy may get temples built or donate part of the money needed for this purpose. Construction of the building over, my idol should be fixed properly in the sanctum sanctorum. Various necessary staff for the regular working of the temple should be appointed. Setting up gardens of flowering plants, arranging festivals on special days etc. are all commendable. Those who offer money or donate land, villages etc. for raising the money needed to run the temple, and do other such sacred deeds will flourish in life. Those who worship me without yearning for anything in return will attain me.

"Those who steal from temples or use the temple fund for own purposes will have to live as lowly creatures for thousands of years. On the other hand, those who build temples, those who help in building them in any way, and those who feel happy about the whole process, will reap the benefit of their good work and thoughts in their lives after death."

In the first nine slokās of the next chapter, Lord Kṛṣṇa tells Uddhava the gist of Jñānayoga. He says:

11.28.1-9: "One should not praise or condemn the nature and deeds of others. He should realize that all are equal in this world, made by the unified action of Prakṛti and Puruṣa. It is clear that one who categorizes others is giving importance to the virtual world; as such, he does not possess true knowledge. When one is asleep, Indriyās do not function; similarly, in ignorance, man sees many people and many things. Saying or even thinking that the good is different from the bad is untrue. There is no duality; what exists is only Brahmam, which is the same as Ātma. Reflections, echoes etc. are unreal; yet in a state of ignorance, they appear to be real. In the same way, belief that the body is real leads to fear of death and life after death. Creation, preservation, and dissolution are done by the Ātma, which is all powerful and is the supreme controller. Materials for creation, the created, and the creator are all the same – the Ātma. Similar is the case with preservation and dissolution. Thus, there exists nothing but the Ātma. Sense of body, Indriyās and Antaḥkaraṇa itself is a result of Māya or ignorance. One who has truly understood this does not praise or criticize others. He journeys in the world with equanimity, like the Sun. Knowing through logical thinking, contemplation and self-experience that this world, which has its origin and end, is unreal, one should move about in the world, free of desires."

At this, Uddhava puts forward his doubts in two verses.

11.28.10-11: "Ātma is devoid of Guṇās. As it is pure, self-luminiscent, and sheath less, it is like fire. It is the seer and the seen. Therefore, it has no Karmās. As the body can be alive only in the presence of the Ātma, it cannot have Karmās on its own, independently. At the same time, it does experience joy and sorrow. So who in reality is involved in Saṁsāram or Kārmik existence?"

To this query, the Lord gives an answer in five verses.

11.28.12-16: "Ātma has no connection to anything. However, the ignorant think that it is connected to the body, mind, the

Indriyās etc. As long as this is the case, Saṁsāram is a reality for them. It is like a man seeing people, and things and going through various emotions in his dream. When he wakes up, he does not care for those unreal materials or experiences. Only one who is egoistic, who is proud of his body, ignoring the real Self, is a slave to grief, joy, anger, greed, desires, fear etc. As soon as the body dies, the Jīvan leaves it, and enters another body. This cycle goes on as long as the Karmās are not fully consumed. Self or the Ātma is never born, neither does it die."

Continuing the discourse, Lord Kṛṣṇa says:

11.28.17-19: "Cutting off ego with the sword of knowledge sharpened by penance, sages travel around the world, absolutely devoid of desires. On developing the ability to differentiate between good and bad as per the Vedās, doing penance, learning from own experiences, analyzing the scriptures logically and coming to the conclusion that whatever was present in the beginning and will be present in the end is the same as what is seen in the middle, and by realizing that the cause of being of everything is time the supreme power, one acquires knowledge. And on gaining knowledge, one loses the sense of many and begins believing in oneness. Gold is gold before it was formed into ornaments, while it is in the form of an ornament, and after it is molten back to its original form. Only its name differs. Same is the case with me and this universe. The power that exists before the origin and after the dissolution of the universe is the same as the power in between, while the universe is existing in its present form."

11.28.20-23: "The states of Jāgṛtāvastha (Wakefulness), Swapnāvastha (Sleep with dreams) and Suṣupti (dreamless deep sleep or slumber) are properties of Manas or the mind. It is the three Guṇās of Satva, Rajas and Tamas that give rise to these three states. In ignorance, Kāraṇam (the cause), Kāryam (the deed done) and Karta (the doer) appear different entities though they are all the same, ultimately speaking. Knowledge is self-luminescent; when one acquires Knowledge, everything becomes crystal clear to him. This is the fourth state of Turīya.

"What is absent in the beginning and the end is absent in the middle too. If it appears to be present, it is just namesake. Similarly, the world appears to be real, though it is unreal. Just like an object becomes visible in the presence of light, the world manifests itself in the light of the cosmic power of the Brahmam. All such knowledge can be gained by the process of elimination, by solid proofs presented in the scriptures, and through a noble guru. Clearing all doubts thus, one should withdraw oneself from his Indriyās and attain absolute bliss."

11.28.24-34: "Ātma is neither the body, nor the Indriyās or the Pancabhūtās, neither mind nor memory, intellect nor ego, neither Prakṛti nor Puruṣa, Prāṇa or Jīvan. One who knows well what the Ātma is, has nothing to do with the material world. Is the Sun affected by clouds? Similarly, Brahmam is not affected by Guṇās. People must consciously avoid Guṇās and their influences as long as they have not become true devotees. Just like diseases not treated properly and fully recur again and again, those who have not gained knowledge fully will be troubled by worldly temptations again and again. However, as they have begun their spiritual journey in the earnest, even if they have to go through the Kārmik cycle over and over, they will progress along the right path due to their experiences in their previous births.

"An ignorant person desirous of the results of his Karmās keeps on performing more and more Karmās till the end of his life. But a Jñāni, who is living in the same world, does not have desires as he is immersed in bliss at all times. Whatever he is doing, whether he is standing or walking or lying down or eating food or urinating or defecating or doing anything else, he knows that it is his body who is the doer. Firmly fixed in the Ātma, he does not experience the dualities affecting his body. He reasons that the whole world is a dream. Ātma is devoid of Guṇās as it is in no way related to Bandha (binding) or Mokṣa (liberation). As long as one is ignorant, one feels that dualities exist. When this ignorance disappears due to the knowledge one gains, truth dawns on him. When there is no sun in the sky, objects cannot be seen in the darkness. When the sun rises, everything becomes visible. The sunlight is making the objects visible, that is all. It is not creating anything.

11.28.35-37: "Ātma is self-luminescent, without birth or death. It cannot be proved by arguments, but has to be experienced to be known. It is noble, is ever existing, is solitary and is witness to everything. It has no second. Any belief contrary to this, propounded by the ignorant who consider themselves wise, is faulty. It originates because of the mind's imagination. The truth is that universe is an illusion. Dreams seem so real while one is dreaming."

11.29.38-44: "While practicing yoga, one may be affected by diseases. These can be cured by Āsanās, Tapas, Mantrās, medicines etc. Some can be cured by meditation, chanting of my names, visits to temples, sticking to diets followed by great sages etc. It is not good to practice yoga for the eight siddhis, because the body is mortal and so efforts to make it supernatural does not make sense. However, if Prāṇāyāma or other such yogic practices are performed as part of attaining spiritual uplift, and as its side effect, the yogi's diseases are cured, there is no harm in it. The prime aim should be to be one with me. One who follows this type of yoga and takes refuge in me, and no one else, will experience pure undiluted joy, for he will never have to face obstacles in his chosen path."

The twenty eighth chapter ends here. The initial six verses of the next chapter are spoken by Uddhava.

11.29.1-6: "Hé Immortal! I wonder why those who cannot control their minds are unable to perform this yoga. Kindly explain to me in simple terms how one can do yoga with ease. Hé lotus-eyed! Even yogis are filled with remorse as they are unable to attain full concentration, even after trying hard. The intelligent, knowing this, take refuge in your feet which shower happiness all around. As a result, they never come under the influence of Māya. On the other hand, Oh Lord of the Universe, the yogis who become proud of their feats are affected by Māya. You are immortal, and you are the God of all gods and goddesses. As you are the well-wisher of all, it is no wonder that you feel one with the helpless. How will anyone who knows that you are the Paramātma, that you are loved by all, and that you are the provider of everything to those who take refuge in you, ignore you and worship someone else for prosperity? You are present inside all and also outside of all; you destroy all evils and show your real shining form to devotees. One cannot repay this favour you bestow on him even in the lifetime of the Creator."

At this juncture, Brahmarṣi Śuka says:

11.29.7: "When Uddhava, full of love and affection, put this question to Kṛṣṇa the supreme Īśwara, for whom the whole universe is a toy, the Lord replied with a beautiful smile."

The next twenty seven verses are spoken by Bhagvān Kṛṣṇa.

11.29.8-19: "Hé Uddhava! I shall tell you happily how a man stable in his dharma conquers death, which is invincible to others. Dedicate all that goes through your mind to me, with pleasure. Do all Karmās thinking of me, for me. Live in holy places where my devotees live. Perform Karmās that my devotees have done. Celebrate temple festivals, songs and dances, bhajans etc. for me, in groups or if affordable, individually.

I am like the sky – present inside and outside every being, yet attached to none. See me as such, as one continuous entity. Knowing that it is I who exist everywhere, in everyone and everything, love and respect all. One who looks at a Brāhmin and a Candāla; a thief and a devotee; the Sun and a spark of fire; the cruel and the kind in the same way is a Vidwān, a knowledgeable person. One who is aware of the fact that I reside everywhere will never be affected by jealousy, unhealthy competition, scorn of others etc. His ego and arrogance vanish instantaneously.

Shun relatives who ridicule others, and leave aside thoughts of the mortal body. Respect without hesitation even animals considered to be lowly, like dogs and donkeys. Do this till the truth that I am omnipresent is fixed in your mind. By reflection and reasoning within, when one realizes that everything is Brahmam, he is cleared of all doubts. For him, differences among the four Varṇās or the four Āśramās do not exist. He is totally dispassionate. I approve of this line of action where one dedicates to me all his thoughts, words and actions."

11.29.20-26: "Hé Uddhava! Not desirous of anything else, one who serves me selflessly is freed from all Guṇās and the resulting doṣās. Even senseless deeds, without any positive outcome, if dedicated to me heartily, become good deeds. A person with a mortal body attaining me, who am immortal, is proof of his astuteness and intelligence. I have told you briefly and also elaborately the essence of Brahmavidya, which even the Devās find difficult to grasp. All those who understand what I have told you will become free of all their doubts. Those who analyze your questions and my answers will attain all the knowledge contained in the Vedās. Whoever respectfully explains to my devotees all that I have told you, I shall show him my true form, even without his asking. He is giving Brahmopadeśa to others; I shall give him the power to know me, residing within himself.

11.29.27-28: "He who daily reads with commitment and devotion this noble and wholesome advice, he who sees me in the light of knowledge, will be freed of all negativity and become absolutely pure. He who listens to this advice with concentration will become my ardent devotee, and will not be bound by Karmās.

11.29.29-31: "Dear friend Uddhava, have you understood Brahmam properly? Have the longing and grief created by your mind been absolved fully? Do not impart this knowledge to those who pretend to be righteous, who do not believe in the Vedās, who are cheats, who do not wish to hear it, and those who do not have any humility. Give it to those devoid of these defects, to those who respect the knowledgeable, to the virtuous, and to the pious downtrodden and women. In fact, give it to all those who are devoted to me.

11.29.32-34: "For those who have understood the veracity of this advice, nothing else remains to be known. For those who have drunk the tastiest celestial Amṛt, no other drink is there, as divine as that. Yogās like Jñānayoga and Karmayoga, Śāstrās like Nītiśastra, trade and agriculture are all useful to man. In the same way, Brahmajñāna is the most useful knowledge to those who want to know the ultimate truth. As and when a person discards all Karmās and surrenders himself unto me in totality, he becomes eligible for Mokṣa, for unification with me."

At this point, Maharṣi Śuka says:

11.29.35-36: "Uddhava, who was listening to Bhagvān in rapt attention all this while folded his hands in reverence and gratitude. His eyes were filled with tears of joy and devotion. As his throat was choking, he could not utter a single word. With deep love and affection, he prostrated himself before Śrī Kṛṣṇa and touched the Lord's lotus feet with his folded hands. Regaining his voice, Uddhava began addressing the noblest of the Yādavās".

11.29.37-40: "Hé Creator of the Creator! The intense darkness which had engulfed me has been driven away by your presence. Will anyone standing near fire be in darkness, feel cold or be afraid? Because of Māya, I was ignorant and in the dark until now. However, you have provided me, your servant, the light of knowledge. Will anyone grateful to you approach others, discarding your sacred feet? On account of your Māya, I was bound by the rope of love to all my relatives and friends till now. Now you have cut that rope yourself, with the weapon of Ātmajñāna. Oh Mahāyogi! Kindly instruct me as to how I can take refuge at your lotus feet at all times. Please accept my respectful salutations."

The last four Ślokās of Uddavagīta are spoken by the Lord.

11.29.41-44: "Hé Uddhava! Now that you have heard with attention all that I told you, you may go to Badri, the blessed Āśram where I had done penance as Nara and Nārāyaṇa. Live there, taking bath and performing the necessary rituals every day in the sacred river Alakananda, consecrated by my feet. You will be wholly purified by this routine. Even the sight of Alakananda at Badari will wash away all sins. Live there wearing bark garments. Do not be interested in any type of pleasure, and eat whatever you get in the forests. Endure extremes of weather, develop all good habits, control your sense organs, keep your intellect firm, and be at peace within. Be well versed in scriptures and learn from your own experiences. Ruminate constantly of what you have heard from me. Dedicate all your thoughts, words and actions to me. Gradually, you will reach levels more advanced than reading of and listening to holy stories, and finally you will attain me."

The divine Uddhavagīta ends here.

Śuka Maharṣi says at this point:

11.29.45-49: "Uddhava, who was enlightened thus by Śrī Kṛṣṇa, circumambulated him, touched the Lord's feet with his head and washed them with tears of devotion, joy and gratitude. Seeing Uddhava sad at separation from him, the Lord gave him his footwear. Uddhava placed them on his head, prostrated himself before Lord Kṛṣṇa and walked away. Fixing Bhagvān Kṛṣṇa in his heart, Uddhava, the greatest devotee of the Lord, went to Badrīkāśram the next day, lived there as instructed by Kṛṣṇa, and finally became one with him.

The absolute truth as explained to Uddhava by the Lord, whose feet are worshipped by all Yogeśwarās, is like nectar churned out of the ocean of knowledge. Anyone who drinks this nectar and lives as per Lord Kṛṣṇa's advice to Uddhava, is liberated from this materialistic world. The Lord has taken out this nectar from the ocean of wisdom, like beetles taking out nectar from flowers. And he has given it to all devotees. This knowledge will drive away all fear of worldly sorrows, including death, for ever. I proffer my salutations to this Puruṣa who has always been there, and whose name is Kṛṣna."

The twenty ninth chapter of the eleventh canto of Śrīmad Bhāgavatam ends here.

Lord Kṛṣṇa, the greatest Ācārya ever, has given the world invaluable advice through Uddhava. Uddhavagīta is very long. It starts towards the end of the sixth chapter and ends with the twenty-ninth chapter. It consists of one thousand forty-two verses in all, and is in the form of a doubt clearing session.

The summary of what Lord Kṛṣṇa told Uddhava was: "An enlightened person is one who sees God in everyone and everything. He has understood that the whole universe is one.

Such a person will never be subject to arrogance, spite, envy or any other such negative feeling. He will be in pursuit of the Supreme Power alone. This is the noblest method of worship. So, shun the thoughts of 'I' and 'mine'. See the whole world as the seat of God. This is the essence of 'Adhyātma yoga'. Practice this and you will become one with me."

Let us offer our salutations here to that great teacher, Lord Kṛṣna, Master of the universe. Om namo Nārāyanāya! Om namo Bhagavate Vāsudevāya!

CHAPTER 15

CONCLUSION

It was when arrangements were being made for everyone to travel to Prabhāsa Tīrtha that Uddhava and Śrī Kṛṣṇa engaged in conversation, which later became famous as Uddhava Gīta. King Parīkṣit now wished to hear from Brahmarṣi Śuka what happened after the Lord concluded his advice to Uddhava. The Maharṣi promptly obliged the king.

The Yādava men along with Kṛṣṇa and Balarāma proceeded to Prabhāsa Tīrtha and reached there by evening. Bath and prayers over, they gave many things in charity to the learned Brāhmins and the needy, and then had dinner. After that, some men got drunk and there erupted a disgusting brawl. In the fight that followed, broken blades of grass containing the iron dust behaved like iron maces! Seeing this, the Yādavās plucked them and used them freely. The fight went on for the whole night. By morning, only the two brothers Kṛṣṇa and Balarāma were alive. The others were all dead.

Convinced that all this was the will of God, Balarāma sat in Padmāsan (the lotus pose) under a nearby Pīpal tree and gave up his physical body by his yogic power.

Time for Kṛṣṇa's ascending heaven was ripe now. He took his

bath, offered prayer in the river Saraswati, entered the forest near Prabhāsa Tīrtha and sat in Vīrāsan (the hero pose) under a tree, his left foot resting on his right thigh. Uddhava visited Kṛṣṇa at that time to receive his blessings. As per the Lord's instruction, he then proceeded to Badrīkāśram for penance.

At that time, Jara the hunter was roaming about in the forest. Looking through the trees, he mistook the sole of Kṛṣṇa's foot for the neck of a deer and sent his special iron-headed arrow at the target. The arrow found its mark. Jara ran to pick the deer up. However, instead of a dead deer, he saw Kṛṣṇa under the tree. The hunter could not contain his sorrow. He fell at Kṛṣṇa's feet and apologized profusely for his grievous sin.

As soon as the Lord pacified the hunter and blessed him, a divine chariot came down from the sky and with Jara in it, rose towards heaven. In the meantime, Dāruka, Kṛṣṇa's charioteer, was grief-stricken on seeing the dead bodies of the Yādavās all over the place. He searched everywhere for his master and ultimately found him under a tree in the forest. The sight of his wounded master melted Dāruka's heart. He got down from Kṛṣṇa's divine chariot, prostrated before him and began crying uncontrollably. The Lord then gave him spiritual advice which calmed him down. Then the chariot in which Dāruka had come slowly rose heavenward. Kṛṣṇa's weapons, which had come down from heaven prior to his war with Jarāsandha, followed suit.

Dāruka was watching all this in great amazement. The Lord blessed him, and told him to go to Dwāraka and inform every one of all that had happened. Also, he should carry Kṛṣṇa's message to Arjuna to take all those left in Dwāraka to Indraprastha. Dāruka prostrated before the Lord and left.

The Lord was now ready to return to Vaikuṇṭha. Knowing this, Devās, Ṛṣis, Apsarās and all other celestials crowded in the sky and showered flowers on Lord Kṛṣṇa. Divine music accompanied heavenly dance. The atmosphere was charged with devotion.

Lord Kṛṣṇa looked skyward. He glanced briefly at each and every one of them, which alone filled their hearts with joy.

Finally, he fixed his eyes on the Creator, standing in the centre of the congregation with folded hands and tears of devotion flowing down his cheeks. Dissolving himself in the Creator through his eyes, and transporting his all-embracing power to Vaikuṇṭha, he closed his eyes. In a fraction of a second, his earthly form vanished from sight like a flash of lightning. Nobody knew where it had gone. Only Lord Brahma and Lord Śiva, with their intrinsic power, saw Kṛṣṇa ascending towards Vaikuṇṭha. All others guessed so. Praising the Lord, they all returned to their respective abodes. Blessed were they who witnessed this astounding Swargārohaṇ. Glory to the omnipresent, omnipotent, omnicious Supreme Being! Let His blessings shower on all of us! Om Śāntih, Śāntih, Śāntihi!

After Lord Kṛṣṇa ascended heaven, Kaliyuga began on earth.

The men and women of Dwāraka who heard of the war within the race and of Kṛṣṇa's Swargārohaṇ from Dāruka the charioteer, rushed to Prabhāsa Tīrtha. There, they saw the dead bodies of their near and dear ones. Many women jumped into the funeral pyres of their husbands. Some men also gave up their mortal bodies in various ways.

Pāṇdavās were grief-stricken at the news. Arjuna came rushing to Dwāraka. He steadied himself remembering what Kṛṣṇa had told him in the battlefield. He did the last rites of all the departed souls. He then took the surviving men, women and children to Indraprastha. He made Vajra, son of Aniruddha, their ruler. Then, making Parīkṣit the ruler of Hastinapura, the Pāṇdavās and Draupadi started on their final journey, the Mahāprasthāna, and ultimately reached heaven.

Liberation is the theme of the eleventh canto. The method of attaining liberation has been described in detail here. Reading or listening to this canto will free human minds of all ignorance. Contemplating on the ideas contained here will result in enlightenment and final release from the vicious circle of birth and death.

Salutations to Hari, the Lord Supreme!

EPILOGUE

Śrīmad Bhāgavatam has always been the most valued book to me. I believe that whatever one needs to know about how to enrich life in this lifetime is given in detail in this holy book. Reading it, one can easily shed one's fear of death too. What more is needed for a stressless life of pure joy?

My first published book was on the stories of Bhāgavatam. That was long back in 2004. Now, in the year 2021, after a few more books, I have had the immense pleasure of coming back to my favourite work - the sacred Bhāgavat Purāna - composed by Maharṣi Vedavyāsa in the distant past. No one knows the exact year of its composition.

Bhagavad-Gīta, part of our great epic Mahābhārata, is well known all over the world. However, the many Gītās incorporated in Śrīmad Bhāgavatam are not widely known. The knowledge contained in these Gītās is philosophical and reflective. It crosses the limits of time and place. This was the reason why I chose to take up this project. Today, I have no words to express my deep sense of contentment and absolute bliss on the completion of this modest work.

I would also like to seek forgiveness from the readrers here, for any inadvertent errors that might have crept into this humble book. My gratefulness to the Lord Supreme at this juncture is boundless. May He shower His blessings on all of us!!!

Om namo Nārāyanāya!

Om namo Bhagavate Vāsudevāya!

Om Śāntih! Śāntih! Śāntihi!

ANNEXURE

A few terms mentioned in Kapilagīta are explained briefly here.

Sabija and Nirbija Yoga

In Sabija Yoga, an object is concentrated upon during meditation. Bija means a seed; this 'seed' is anything that exists in Nature. A seed can be any gross object like a rock, or a subtle object like a thought, or an emotion.

In Nirbija Yoga, on the other hand, there is no object, or seed, to meditate upon. The seeker himself is the object. He wants to see and experience the reality of himself.

Aṣṭāngayoga (The Eight Limbs of Yoga)

Patanjali's eight-fold path of yoga offers guidelines for a meaningful and purposeful life. It enhances moral and ethical conduct and self-discipline.

1. Yama

   The first limb, yama, deals with one's ethical standards and sense of integrity, focusing on our behavior. The five yamas are:

Ahimsa: non-violence

Satya: truthfulness

Asteya: non-stealing

Brahmacarya: continence

Aparigraha: non-covetousness

2. Niyama

   Niyama, the second limb, is all about self-discipline and spiritual practices. The five niyamas are:

Śauca: cleanliness

Saṁtoṣa: contentment

Tapas: spiritual austerities

Swādhyāya: study of the sacred scriptures and of one's self

Īśwara Praṇidhāṇa: surrender to God

3. Āsana

   Āsanās, the postures practiced in yoga, comprise the third limb. By practicing āsanās, we develop the habit of discipline and the ability to concentrate, both of which are necessary for meditation.

4. Prānāyāma

   Generally translated as breath control, this fourth stage incorporates techniques designed to master the process of respiration. Prāṇāyāma consists of three parts. Pūraka or inhalation, Kumbhaka or retention, and Recaka or exhalation. The ideal ratio of time period for these three activities is 1:4:2 respectively.

   It is important to realize that there exists a connection among breath, mind, and emotions. Prāṇāyāma improves resistance to diseases and rejuvenates the body along with increasing the life span of the practitioner. At a spiritual level, it helps to keep the mind calm and increases the power of concentration.

5. Pratyāhāra

   Pratyāhāra, the fifth limb, means trying consciously to draw our awareness away from outside stimuli and the external world in general. By doing this, we direct our attention internally. Pratyāhāra makes us step back and look at ourselves. This is a step towards realizing the Self.

6. Dhāraṇa

   Pratyāhāra sets the stage for Dhāraṇa, or concentration. After getting rid of external distractions, the practitioner can now deal with the distractions of the mind itself. Concentration can be done on one object like the image of a deity, or silent repetition of a sound. Dhāraṇa gradually leads to the next stage of meditation.

7. Dhyāna

   This seventh stage of Dhyāna is meditation which involves continuous concentration. The difference between Dhāraṇa and Dhyāna is that in the former, the attention is on one point, while in the latter, at this stage, the mind is still and there is no thought.

8. Samādhi

   This is the eighth and last stage of Patanjali's Aṣṭānga Yoga. Samādhi is a state of ecstasy. At this stage, the practitioner transcends the self completely. He or she is connected to the entire creation and experiences the absolute bliss of being at one with the Universe. Samādhi, which is a state of enlightenment, cannot be expressed in words. It can only be experienced.

About Indus Source Books

Indus Source Books is a niche, independent book publisher in Mumbai passionately committed to publishing good and relevant literature. We believe that books are one of the most important mediums of communication and we seek to bring out publications that help to serve the community and the world we live in.

At Indus Source Books, we celebrate the diverse spiritual traditions, culture, and history of the world and present it to our readers in a contemporary format that retains its essential flavour: "Indian Spirit, Universal Wisdom".

Use the QR code below to visit our website www.indussource.com for more details.

reSource

Indus Source Books
PO Box 6194
Malabar Hill PO
Mumbai 400006
India
www.indussource.com
info@indussource.com